Romey J Barnes

GUIDELINES FOR SENSORY ANALYSIS IN FOOD PRODUCT DEVELOPMENT AND QUALITY CONTROL

GUIDELINES FOR SENSORY ANALYSIS IN FOOD PRODUCT DEVELOPMENT AND QUALITY CONTROL

Edited by

David H. Lyon
*Head of Department of Sensory Quality
and Food Acceptability
Campden Food and Drink Research Association*

Mariko A. Francombe
*Head of Sensory Analysis
RHM Research and Engineering Ltd*

Terry A. Hasdell
*Manager, Sensory Research Section
United Biscuits Group Research and
Development Centre*

Ken Lawson
*Sensory Analyst/Food Technologist
Mars Confectionery UK Ltd*

CHAPMAN & HALL
London · New York · Tokyo · Melbourne · Madras

Published by Chapman & Hall, 2–6 Boundary Row, London SE1 8HN

Chapman & Hall, 2–6 Boundary Row, London SE1 8HN, UK

Van Nostrand Reinhold Inc., 115 5th Avenue, New York NY10003, USA

Chapman & Hall Japan, Thomson Publishing Japan, Hirakawacho Nemoto Building, 6F, 1–7–11 Hirakawa-cho, Chiyoda-ku, Tokyo 102, Japan

Chapman & Hall Australia, Thomas Nelson Australia, 102 Dodds Street, South Melbourne, Victoria 3205, Australia

Chapman & Hall India, R. Seshadri, 32 Second Main Road, CIT East, Madras 600 035, India

First edition 1992

© 1992 David H. Lyon, Mariko A. Francombe, Terry A. Hasdell and Ken Lawson

Typeset in Palatino 10/12 pt by Columns Design & Production Services Ltd, Reading
Printed in Great Britain by St Edmundsbury Press, Suffolk

ISBN 0 412 42950 0   0 442 31553 8 (USA)

A catalogue record for this book is available from the British Library

Library of Congress Cataloging-in-Publication data available

Contents

viii   *Contents*

Preface

Sensory analysis is not new to the food industry, but its application as a basic tool in food product development and quality control has not been given the recognition and acceptance it deserves. This, we believe, is largely due to the lack of understanding about what sensory analysis can offer in product research, development and marketing, and a fear that the discipline is 'too scientific' to be practical. To some extent, sensory scientists have perpetuated this fear with a failure to recognize the constraints of industry in implementing sensory testing procedures. These guidelines are an attempt to redress the balance.

Of course, product 'tasting' is carried out in every food company: it may be the morning tasting session by the managing director, competitor comparisons by the marketeers, tasting by a product 'expert' giving a quality opinion, comparison of new recipes from the product development kitchen, or on-line checking during production. Most relevant, though, is that the people responsible for the tasting session should know why the work is being done, and fully realize that if it is not done well, then the results and conclusions drawn, and their implications, are likely to be misleading. If, through the production of these guidelines, we have influenced some people sufficiently for them to re-evaluate what they are doing, and why, we believe our efforts have been worthwhile.

The authors of these *Guidelines for Sensory Analysis in Food Product Development and Quality Control* are all practical sensory analysts with a wide range of experience in using sensory analysis in industrial situations. Our numbers include the sensory analysts working in major UK food companies and sensory scientists from the Campden Food and Drink Research Association. We are all members of the Campden Sensory Evaluation Working Group, an active forum for the discussion of new research and the exchange of practical experiences in the use of sensory analysis. The recommendations we offer are all based on many years of practical experience, and we intend to use these guidelines widely throughout our own companies to help our colleagues attain a greater understanding of the usefulness of sensory analysis techniques when applied in a controlled and appropriate manner.

In considering the need for a guideline document, we were aware of no other publication which has been specifically designed to help both the individual carrying out the test and those within industry using sensory analysis. It is our opinion that both would benefit from a clearer explanation of the role of sensory analysis in product development and quality control. We had as our objective, therefore, the need to prepare a document which would promote the use of sensory analysis within the food industry, and encourage the use of sensory analysis as an integral part of product development and quality control.

The main part of the guidelines has been written to follow a logical sequence of questions which might be asked before embarking on sensory analysis. We have tried to make the layout user-friendly, with a question and answer format that can be dipped into as and when guidance is required on particular issues. We have included brief descriptions of some of the most widely used sensory tests and provided the reader with details of where they might find more information about particular tests, if we believe they are adequately documented elsewhere. References to suitable and helpful literature are given together with a glossary of terms. We have drawn on our experiences to provide case histories and examples of when sensory tests have proved useful in particular situations.

Finally, we hope to have illustrated that good sensory practice is not just a question of resource, and that everyone will gain some help for their company when using the guidelines. Whatever the size of the company, whatever the standard of the sensory facilities, if the approach takes into account the ideas we have offered in these guidelines, we are sure that it will result in greater confidence in sensory testing, and greater reliability in the application of the results of sensory analysis.

Contributors

Zoë V. Baines, PhD
Sensory Research Scientist
United Biscuits Research and Development Centre

Zoë Baines is a graduate of the University of London. She gained a PhD for her work on 'The influence of food texture on flavour and taste perception' at Cranfield Institute of Technology in 1988. Her thesis won the Lord Kings Norton Medal for the best PhD thesis submitted at Cranfield in the 1988/89 academic year. Zoë joined the research group at United Biscuits in 1989 and has been involved in sensory testing of company products using both trained and untrained assessors.

Pamela K. Beyts
Sensory Evaluation Manager
Tate and Lyle Speciality Sweeteners

After obtaining her Honours degree in Chemistry from St. Andrews University and a Masters Degree in Food Science from the University of Leeds, Pamela spent three years as a food technologist carrying out new product development for Schweppes International. Following this, she spent nine years as Sensory Evaluation Manager at Tate and Lyle. During this time, she led a team of sensory scientists concerned with assessing the sensory characteristics of new food products and ingredients.

Recently, Pamela has established her own consultancy, and is now proprietor of Sensory Dimensions, an independent company carrying out contract research for the food and drink industry.

Roland P. Carpenter
Unilever Research, Colworth Laboratory

Roland Carpenter obtained an Honours degree in Biochemistry at Exeter College, Oxford, and spent a further
three years researching protein structure, before taking up
an appointment with Unilever Research in 1970.

For the following decade, he worked on a variety of
product and process development projects in fish and meat
technology. Roland joined the Sensory Analysis Group, and
now manages the Sensory Resource, which undertakes a
wide-ranging product evaluation programme, aided by
modern, comprehensive computing facilities.

Roland is a member of the Sensory and Consumer Science
Group Committee of the SCI, London.

Jennifer D. Cloke, PhD
Section Leader of Food Properties
Londreco Ltd

Jennifer Cloke graduated with a first-class Honours degree
from Nottingham University. She obtained her Masters
degree and PhD in Food Science from the University of
Minnesota, USA. She has worked at Londreco Ltd, a
research and development company belonging to Nestlé, for
six years and currently heads a research team whose
interests include sensory analysis.

Jennifer is Secretary of the Food Additives Group of the
Institute of Food Science and Technology. She is also a
member of SCI, the Institute of Food Technologists, the
Royal Society of Health and the American Association of
Cereal Chemists.

Janet S. Colwill, PhD
Senior Research Officer
Campden Food and Drink Research Association

Janet Colwill graduated from Leeds University with a
degree in Home Economics and Public Media and obtained
her PhD from Huddersfield Polytechnic in Catering Sci-
ences. Janet joined Campden in 1986 where she has
established consumer research and acceptability studies.

Janet is active in research projects both with consumers
and with trained assessors, and is involved in establishing

quality standards for the UK food industry. She has written many papers and presented at international symposia on aspects of sensory analysis, consumer acceptability and quality control.

Ann Duffield
Sensory Analyst
Kraft General Foods

Ann Duffield has been involved in sensory analysis for over 20 years during her career at Kraft General Foods, initially as a panel member and latterly as Sensory Analyst. Working in research and development, her responsibility was mainly to coffee development, but also included training and advisory support for quality control.

For several years, Ann was Secretary of the Sensory Panel of the Food Group of SCI. Ann retired from Kraft General Foods in 1990 to take up a second career outside the food industry.

Mariko A. Francombe
Head of Sensory Analysis
RHM Research and Engineering Ltd

Mariko Francombe graduated in Microbiology from the University of Bristol and started her career in sensory analysis when she joined the AFRC Institute of Food Research – Bristol Laboratory (then the Meat Research Institute) in 1981. Since 1986, she has led the Sensory Analysis section at the central research and engineering company for the Rank Hovis McDougall Group.

Mariko was Chairman of the Sensory Evaluation Working Group, responsible for developing these guidelines, from 1989 to 1991. She is also a committee member of the SCI Sensory and Consumer Science Group.

Nerys M. Griffiths
Deputy Head of Sensory Quality and Food Acceptability
Campden Food and Drink Research Association

Nerys Griffiths graduated in Plant Biochemistry, then carried out research on phenolic browning both in tobacco and potatoes. In 1965 she joined a multidisciplinary team working on odour description and classification; this work provided the basis for much of the European profile analysis. During this time, she gained her training in sensory analysis working with Roland Harper, the 'father' of British sensory analysis. Nerys set up the original sensory facility at the Institute of Food Research, Norwich to investigate the source and nature of taints and naturally occurring flavour problems, as well as sensory measurements related to poultry processing.

Since joining Campden, Nerys has expanded her interests in packaging and perceived shelf-life, and is working closely with industry to increase the objectivity of sensory tests used on line and in quality control.

Terry A. Hasdell
Manager, Sensory Research Section
United Biscuits, Group Research and Development Centre

Terry Hasdell has been working in food research for the past 33 years and specifically in sensory analysis for the past 24 years. His early experience was gained at Colworth Laboratory of Unilever Research. In 1973, he joined United Biscuits to set up and manage the Sensory Analysis Section. As the company has expanded, the size of the section and the scope of its activities and products have increased dramatically.

Terry is a committee member of the SCI Sensory and Consumer Science Group and a member of the BSI committee on sensory methodology.

Merille Hughes
Sensory Analyst
Showerings Ltd

Merille Hughes has been working in the field of flavour application and development for six years. Merille worked for two leading flavour houses before joining Showerings Ltd in 1989 to develop the company's sensory analysis function.

Merille is an Associate of the British Society of Flavourists.

Ken Lawson
Sensory Analyst/Food Technologist
Mars Confectionery UK Ltd

Ken Lawson is a graduate of South London Polytechnic College and has worked at Mars Confectionery Ltd for 18 years. For the past ten years, he has been involved in the creation of a modern sensory facility which is engaged in the use of advanced sensory techniques, including computerized collection and statistical modelling of sensory data. He has extensive practical experience of sensory analysis for product development and quality control, and its use in interpretation of consumer data.

Ken is the Chairman of the Sensory Evaluation Working Group.

Jeannette A. Lynch
Sensory Analyst
Londreco Ltd

Jeannette Lynch has been working in the field of sensory analysis for the past ten years. She trained in the sensory evaluation department of the Institute of Food Research – Bristol Laboratory and has since worked for a market research company. At Londreco, a research and development company for Nestlé, she manages the sensory evaluation work on products being developed and improved; where she uses a variety of methods including consumer panels.

David H. Lyon, FIFST
Head of Department of Sensory Quality and Food Acceptability
Campden Food and Drink Research Association

David Lyon is a graduate of the University of Reading and has been working in the field of sensory analysis for the past 12 years. He currently leads a research team looking at new and applied sensory methods, including sensory quality assurance, improved techniques for collecting consumer data and the use of trained panels and consumers for product optimization and product development purposes.

David is Chairman of the European Sensory Network, formed to promote the practical applications of sensory analysis and to provide a forum for international cooperation in sensory research. David is a Fellow of the Institute of

Food Science and Technology, Chairman of the SCI Sensory & Consumer Science Group, a member of the BSI committee on sensory methodology and a member of the editorial board of the *Journal of Food Quality and Preference*.

Jean A. McEwan, PhD
Senior Research Officer
Campden Food and Drink Research Association

Jean McEwan joined Campden in 1988 after completing her PhD thesis on methodology and new applications in food acceptance research at the University of Reading. Previously, she obtained her degree in Statistics at the University of Glasgow.

Whilst responsible for statistics and computing in the Department of Sensory Quality and Food Acceptability, Jean continues her interests in consumer research, and is involved in the management of several projects in this area. Her work includes the application of alternative statistical methods for consumer data, and the investigation of methods for relating sensory, consumer and physical/ chemical data. Jean has written many scientific papers and presented at several international symposia.

Anne Olivant
Technical Development Manager
Beecham Products (now CPC (UK) Ltd, Ambrosia Creamery)

Anne Olivant is a graduate of the National College of Food Technology, University of Reading and a Member of the Institute of Food Science and Technology.

Following graduation, Anne has worked in the field of product development and quality control and currently leads the Ambrosia Research and Development Department in new product and process development.

Margaret A. Reynolds
Sensory Analyst
Walkers Crisps Ltd

Margaret Reynolds has been involved in the quality control and quality assurance of both food and non-food products for over nine years, and has specialized in sensory analysis since graduating from Newcastle Polytechnic in 1986. In her present position, she is responsible for the sensory facility and applying sensory techniques for research and development, marketing and production. She is particularly involved in establishing effective sensory testing at production level.

Margaret is a member of the SCI Sensory and Consumer Science Group Committee.

Trevor M. Stevens
Senior Product Services Co-ordination Manager
Rowntree Mackintosh

Trevor Stevens is a chemist by training with specialist application to flavour and colour chemistry within the Company's UK operation. Trevor was responsible for setting up and subsequent operation of a UK sensory network and currently oversees its use, continued expansion and development within the Company's technical function.

Trevor represents the Biscuit, Cake, Chocolate and Confectionery Alliance on the Food and Drink Federation Flavourings Working Group, and is a member of the Essential Oils Sub Committee of the Royal Society of Chemistry. He is a Member of the Institute of Food Science and Technology, a licentiate of the Royal Society of Chemistry and a Fellow of the British Society of Flavourists.

L. John Taylor
Consumer Science Section
Unilever Research

John Taylor is a graduate of the University of Southampton and has worked in the field of sensory analysis and consumer research for 18 years. He has wide experience of the application of sensory and consumer research techniques in the development of food products and of the integration of sensory data with consumer and instrumental data.

Nick Townhill
Development Manager
Showerings Ltd

Nick Townhill is a graduate of the University of Leicester and has worked within the technical function at Showerings for 15 years. Working initially within Quality Control, Nick now heads the Development Section responsible for the development and introduction of new processes, products and packaging. Nick is responsible for the training and monitoring of Showerings' sensory panel and for compiling flavour specifications for each of the company's products.

Nick is an Associate of the British Society of Flavourists.

Ann C. Wilson
Manager – Sensory Evaluation
Quaker Oats Ltd

Ann is a graduate of the University College, London. In the past she has worked in marketing research with particular interests in new product research. Ann currently directs the UK sensory operation for Quaker Oats.

Ann is a member of the committee of the SCI Sensory and Consumer Science Group.

Introduction

Perhaps you believe that sensory analysis may have something to offer your company, either as an internal function or as a service bought in on a contract basis. Perhaps you have been asked to set up your own sensory testing service and are looking not only for guidelines, but also for arguments to justify and sell your involvement in commercial projects. Perhaps you are studying sensory analysis and are looking to see how it is best applied in the food industry. Whoever you are, and whatever your purpose for delving into this book, here is the chance to explore a few fundamental questions which may be going through your mind.

- What is it and what does it tell us?
- Why should we use sensory analysis?
- How does sensory analysis help?
- What are the benefits of using sensory analysis?
- How do we get started?

What is it and what does it tell us?

Sensory analysis is the definition and scientific measurement of the attributes of a product perceived by the senses: sight, sound, smell, taste and touch. This frequently cited broad definition embraces both qualitative and quantitative approaches, and does not discriminate between whether the sensory attributes are being assessed by consumers or trained assessors, or whether objective or

subjective sensory questions are being asked about products. It is interesting that 'in the trade' there has been a
perception that sensory analysis, with its roots in science
and the laboratory, is only about objective sensory questions and quantitative answers and that subjective questions of quality lie in the separate realm of consumer
research, led by marketeers and social scientists. Perhaps
the definition of sensory analysis has not been specific
enough, or perhaps the narrower interpretation of what
sensory analysis is about has been necessary in its early
years to identify it as a different approach and to protect its
scientific credibility.

Either way, nowadays there is more integration of what
were traditionally seen as sensory analysis and consumer
research methods into an array of complementary product
tests focusing on sensory questions. This has been encouraged by customer choice-driven markets and the need
to identify the customers' ideals and expectations of sensory
quality to help set sensory targets in the design and
development of products. So now we are growing to fulfil
our broad definition of sensory analysis whilst at the same
time maintaining the rigorous approaches of our scientific
origin!

Sensory analysis answers questions of quality in three
main areas, as follows.

Description

What does the product taste like? What are its perceived
sensory characteristics? How is one product different from
another in quality? How does a change in process/
formulation/packaging/storage conditions affect its attributes?

Discrimination

Would people notice the difference? Would people detect
this? How many would discriminate/detect this? Is this
different? How great is the difference? Is this the same as
that?

Preference or hedonics

How much do people like this? Is it acceptable? Is it as good as another product? Is this an improvement over another product? Which attributes are liked? Is it preferred?

Why should we use sensory analysis?

In food companies, manufacturing or retail, product tasting is practically a daily occurrence. Reasons for looking at products are manifold: maintaining awareness of company or competitor products; promoting company products to potential customers; demonstrating latest products to the sales team; keeping the project team or management up to date on product development progress or production issues; seeking a customer's approval; deciding on changes to products; checking that product quality matches a target or meets a specification. All except the last two purposes are largely exercises in communications, maintaining awareness and promoting products to secure management or customer approval. The exceptions are two examples of where sensory information is required to make decisions about product quality. When *ad hoc* opinions, observations and comments made at informal tastings become major influences in the life history of a product, decisions are made about sensory quality in circumstances which are not designed for, and often militate against, obtaining good sensory information. The quality of the sensory information, of course, affects the quality of the decisions. That is not to say that sensory analysis should take over any decision-making about quality, or replace tasting for awareness, or promotional reasons, but we believe that sensory analysis should be used to provide the best possible information to help make all these business activities more effective.

So, what are the problems associated with obtaining sensory information in informal tasting sessions? Commonly, they fall into the following five categories: bias; subjectivity; wrong assessors; poor control of variables; patchy information.

There is the problem of *bias*. Judgements may be biased, for example by an assessor's preconceptions of a product if sensory testing is not carried out 'blind', or by his or her vested interest in the outcome of the assessment. Order of tasting products and the influence of other dominant opinions, such as those of the most senior person present, are other sources of bias in these situations.

Subjective judgements are often made inappropriately. It is easier, in the absence of formal guidelines, training and clearly defined references, to say how much you like a product, rather than analyse its quality. Of course, sometimes to ask about liking of the product is the legitimate question, but what information does this give you if you want to know how to improve product quality? Also, are the right people making the judgement of liking? Are the people giving their opinions representative enough, in number and type, of the product user or customer? Usually not. This approach is often justified by saying that companies know their customers, but is consumer research available to describe in sensory terms what the customer does expect from the company's product? At the tasting session, is the question asked and answered in terms of what the customer would like? More often opinions given are personal ones.

The issue of the *right people making the assessment* also extends into the more objective and analytical sensory questions. Are the people assessing the products sufficiently sensitive to the relevant food stimuli? Are they discriminating? Are they trained or otherwise able to be analytical in approach, and articulate about their perceptions?

Product presentation and tasting environment also influence the outcome of a tasting session. The ability of people to judge food is affected by distractions like noise, including talking, intrusive odours, excessive heat or cold or other discomfort, so it is important to rule these out as much as possible. Control over the sampling of products is important. Often participants help themselves to portions of product in any order, and the resulting assessment varies between individuals partly because the actual samples of product differed in size, composition, or serving temperature.

The last point is the problem of *patchy information*. Informal tasting sessions have not usually been planned to answer clear objectives with structured questionnaires. Information forthcoming is sometimes not recorded, or assessors simply write comments. In the absence of defined and common terminology, the interpretation of comments is risky, and without a structured direction of the assessors' attention to particular aspects, not everything is noticed by everyone and thus the product picture is incomplete.

How does sensory analysis help?

It tackles all the issues raised in this product assessment minefield, offering scientific approaches to obtain complete and appropriate information about product sensory quality. Sensory analysis is all about ways of removing or taking into account sources of unwanted error through control of environment and sampling, through good experimental design, and by selecting the most appropriate 'instruments' to make the measurements. It is about asking the right questions and taking into account what we know about human perception.

What are the benefits of using sensory analysis?

Several of the sensory questions are asked about products whether new or old, company or competitor, by managing directors, marketeers, factory managers, technical, development and research staff, quality managers and production staff alike. They are questions which are important to a food business, as getting the right answers cumulatively contributes to product success in the market-place. We urge you to consider the cost of getting the answers wrong! At worst, the product fails immediately or gradually because it does not deliver customers' expectations of quality. Problems of communication and decision-making over products based on poor information may lead to wasted time, effort and material costs in development, wasted consumer research, even wasted production. We believe sensory analysis integrated into the business will help to shorten development lead times and contribute to a better understanding of product behaviour. At the same time, using sensory analysis portrays professionalism which benefits the company in its dealings with its customers.

How do we get started?

First of all, the venture must be supported by senior management and someone must be made visibly responsible for sensory analysis in the company. The next thing will be to identify suitable facilities. Ideally, this would include a food preparation area, specially designed sensory testing booths, a briefing and discussion area, and a microcomputer. However, a starting point could be the use of existing facilities, as long as products could be prepared and served hygienically in standardized conditions, and the assessors could do their tests independently and quietly in a room which is free of extraneous odours and distractions and is evenly illuminated. Sensory panels will then need to be recruited. Potential trained assessors will be screened for sensory ability and a register drawn up of assessors willing to participate in tests where specific selection and training is not required. The new sensory analyst will need to learn the basic tests and data analysis with guidance from this book and its references. It would be helpful if a statistician were at hand for advice, but there are sensory data analysis packages for microcomputers available for the standard tests.

Finally, there is putting it all into practice. We hope our guidelines help with this, but there are some things to say at the outset. Essentially, keep it simple and follow these golden rules.

- Be clear on test objectives. Think about the possible outcome of tests and identify action standards if possible.
- Do not make things too complicated for your assessors. In considering your objectives break complex questions into a series of simple ones. Do one test at a time to avoid bias and confusion.
- Recruit the right assessors for your test.
- Create the best environment you can for the analysis.
- Minimize sources of error from samples.
- Do not try to assess too many samples at once. Break them into small sets and test with a rest in between.
- Design your test to minimize error and bias from assessors.
- Ensure your assessors are clear on their task.

• Know how to analyse and present your results for best effect.

We wish you every success!

What is sensory analysis used for? 1

Sensory analysis is used to establish difference and to characterize and measure sensory attributes of products, or to establish whether product differences are acceptable or unacceptable and noticeable to the consumer. In product development and quality control, understanding, determining and evaluating the sensory characteristics of products are important in many applications. These include shelf-life studies, product matching, product mapping, product specification and quality assurance, product reformulation, testing for taint potential and determining product acceptability. This chapter discusses these main applications in more detail. Questions at the end of each section are typical examples which might be asked of the sensory analyst when addressing any one of these applications. Tests to answer these questions are discussed in detail in the guidelines. The reader should bear these questions in mind when deciding which test is most appropriate.

According to United Kingdom (UK) and European Community (EC) food law, most prepackaged foods must be labelled by the manufacturer with a 'use by' or a 'best before' date. (Food Labelling Regulations: HMSO, 1984; 1989; 1990). As from 1 January 1991 it is now an offence in the UK to sell products which have passed the 'use by' date. Obviously, therefore, manufacturers must be able accurately to predict the shelf-life of their products to ensure that the consumer receives the product in satisfactory condition, and that there is sufficient 'unexpired' shelf-life for normal distribution and retail purposes. What constitutes 'shelf-life' or 'minimum durability' is referred to in the UK Food Labelling Regulations (HMSO, 1984) as 'up to and including the date which a food can reasonably be expected to retain its specific properties if properly stored'. While this is open to interpretation, it clearly implies that a product must not have undergone unacceptable changes in its sensory characteristics, and that storage conditions will affect the rate of deterioration.

Many factors are likely to affect the sensory attributes of products during shelf-life and, ultimately, the acceptability of the product to the consumer. A few examples are given below.

Temperature

Frozen vegetables stored at low temperatures (−25°C (−13°F) to −30°C (−22°F)) have a longer shelf-life than vegetables stored at higher temperatures (−12°C (10.4°F) to −18°C (−0.4°F)). The sensory characteristics of products stored at higher frozen temperatures deteriorate more rapidly than those of products stored at lower frozen temperatures (Lyon *et al.*, 1988).

Light

Oxidation of certain products occurs more rapidly in the presence of light. Amongst other things, oxidation causes discolouration which affects the acceptability of the product.

Packaging

Certain packaging films act as an oxygen barrier and will retard lipid oxidation which gives rise to rancidity.

Atmosphere

The presence of carbon dioxide and low oxygen within packs will reduce the rate of microbiological growth on meat and thereby reduce spoilage and increase the shelf-life. Humid conditions shorten the shelf-life of dry products which may become soft and therefore unacceptable.

Storage, distribution and retail procedures

Storage in the factory or warehouse must be under conditions which will not cause product deterioration. Transport and distribution must follow procedures which will not cause damage to the product or the pack during handling, and products in retail stores must be displayed under optimum conditions.

In considering shelf-life studies, it is therefore important to decide whether the limit on shelf-life is the point at which a detectable change in the sensory characteristics occurs, bearing in mind that most products will change to some degree under normal storage conditions, or the point at which a detectable change becomes unacceptable to the consumer. In fact, a precise working definition will vary from product to product and company to company, but the nature of the definition will determine the approach and type of sensory test to use.

Typical questions

- How long can this product be stored before the sensory quality noticeably changes?
- How does the sensory quality change with storage?
- How long before the sensory quality changes make the product unacceptable?

1.3 Product matching

Sensory analysis can be used in product matching to compare and modify the sensory characteristics of one product to be in line with the sensory characteristics of another, similar product. The need for product matching may come from several sources. For example, the request may come from the production department to help to match main plant to pilot plant production, from the marketing department to compare and match an own brand with a brand leader, or from product development with the request to match formulations using ingredients from different suppliers.

Usually in product matching the 'target' product has been identified, as in the examples above. Objective or analytical approaches to sensory analysis are therefore the most appropriate, using principally the techniques of descriptive profiling. In other cases, for example in matching a marketing concept derived from consumer focus groups (Greenbaum, 1988) or projective methods (Oppenheim, 1966), it will be necessary constantly to refer to consumer views through market research trials, or, more effectively, to utilize predictive statistical modelling to target the optimization process (Thomson, 1988). Some of these approaches utilize product-mapping techniques, an example of which is explained and described in detail as a case history in Chapter 10.

Typical questions

Target setting
- How is the ideal product described?
- What are the key attributes to meet consumers' expectations of the concept?
- What are the main sensory attributes affecting liking for the product?
- What are the main attributes of this type of product?
- What are the attributes of the benchmark product?

Screening versus target/benchmark
- Does this sample match the target profile?
- Is this sample perceptibly different from the benchmark?
- If the sample differs, in what way does it differ? How can it be made more like the target profile?
- Have the changes brought the product closer to the target?
- Which sample is closest to the target?

1.4 Product mapping

The analysis of sensory profile data using multivariate statistical techniques (Piggott, 1986; Thomson, 1988) enables products to be placed on to a product-attribute map or a product-market map. The 'distances' between the products on the map relate to the size and the nature of the difference in sensory characteristics of the products. Product-attribute mapping is particularly useful in product matching as described above, as it clearly indicates the attributes which differentiate the samples. Product mapping, where sensory profiles are produced for a range of products in the market place (also known as market mapping), helps to identify product position in respect to competitive products, and to identify gaps in the product range which may be successfully filled by new product development.

One of the major difficulties in the development and control of food products can be the communication interface between marketing and technical functions within companies. Product matching and product mapping, when used at that interface, are invaluable in ensuring that company resources are directed to maximum benefit. An example of product mapping is given in the case history in Chapter 10.

Typical questions

- What are the attributes of products already on the market?
- What are the sensory differences among products?
- What are the attributes of the most and least successful products, or of products which are most and least liked?
- Are there gaps in the sensory map?
- Which combinations of attributes comprise a consumer's ideal product?
- Have the changes brought the product closer to the target or benchmark?

1.5 Specifications and quality control

The use of product specifications in the manufacture and supply of food items is essential in normal commercial practice. A widely used definition of quality in this context is 'The collection of features and characteristics of a product or service that confer its ability to satisfy stated or implied needs' (ISO, 1990). If considered closely in the sensory context, this definition can be seen to comprise two parts: the first includes the objective sensory factors related to the product (. . .the collection of features. . .), while the second refers to the subjective sensory factors related to the user or consumer of the goods (. . .to satisfy stated or implied need. . .). A definition of a product sensory quality specification would then be 'A document which clearly identifies the important characteristics of a product, and which can act as a basis of agreement between the buyer and the seller of that product'.

A product specification will, of course, contain many characteristics which are not related to sensory factors, such as labelling requirements and standards of fill, and will cover the sensory related aspects to a greater or lesser extent depending upon the product. The five quality parameters which can be most easily associated with sensory factors are appearance (colour), flavour (and odour), texture, size, and freedom from defects.

Product-orientated sensory specifications may be voluntary trading documents between buyer and seller, recommended national or international trading documents, or statutory national or international trading regulations. The advantage of voluntary trading specifications is that commercial decisions can be more easily taken as to whether a product is suitable for a particular market. However, once agreement has been reached, voluntary specifications will usually be binding as part of the contract agreed between buyer and seller.

Sensory specifications are derived through agreement, using product quality ranges to determine the acceptable and unacceptable limits of sensory characteristics. The product sensory characteristics associated with these limits of acceptability are described in an objective manner and are used to form the basis of a product grading system. The sensory analyst may play a key role in defining sensory characteristics in an objective way, and in training quality control staff in the interpretation and implementation of the grading system following the principles described in these guidelines. Quality control staff should always be trained to be objective and consistent, with experience playing a large part in their ability to recognize when a product falls outside the normal acceptable range for their company. For example, they will need to recognize the acceptable range of within batch and between batch product variation, which can only come about through frequent exposure to the total range.

Typical questions

- What is the target specification?
- Does this product match the target specification?
- What variation in quality is to be expected? What is the normal variation in each attribute?
- Is there a noticeable difference between the test and standard?

Every company will engage in product reformulation at some stage in the life of a product. Even those companies who rightly claim to use 'original recipes' are subjected to the same modern legislation as everyone else, and additives or ingredients available when the original recipe was conceived may no longer be available. Moreover, equipment wears out and new process lines have to be installed, the traditional supplier may no longer be reliable or available, the standard ingredient has become too expensive, or a competitor may have introduced a 'me too' product which is taking an increasing market share. All these problems will require some degree of reformulation either to change or to maintain the current market position.

Sensory analysis will be able to help companies in product reformulation. Descriptive profiling can characterize changes due to ingredient or process substitutions, and can identify when competitor products have successfully matched a product formulation to threaten the market share. This can be effectively combined with product knowledge from experts, knowledge about production variations, and information from consumers on trends and fashions which may influence acceptability.

Typical questions

- If the recipe/process/package were changed, how would quality be affected?
- Does this change cause the product to vary outside the normal range?
- Does this change make a noticeable difference?
- By how much can the sensory characteristics be changed before liking for the product is affected?

Taints are odours or flavours which are foreign to the product and, if present, are likely to lead to consumer complaints. Precautions must be taken at all stages of production and distribution to ensure that products do not come into contact with substances likely to impart a taint, or that products are put into a situation which might give rise to a taint. Fully documented examples of taints in industrial situations are difficult to come by, as companies are often unwilling publicly to debate their experiences on this very sensitive issue. Most companies would agree, however, that there are situations which are common to most food manufacturers and which must be regarded as a potential source of taint. These include the following:

- Contact with painted surfaces or the solvents from paint used on floors, walls, ceilings or equipment, not necessarily only in the immediate vicinity of the food.
- Flooring in the food preparation or storage areas. There may be a particular problem with curing agents used when new floors are laid or old floors repaired.
- Disinfectants used on the processing line directly, or to clean equipment, containers, lorries, floors, etc. In general, disinfectants should always be stored away from the preparation area and never contain chlorophenols.
- Packaging used for the ingredients or the final product. In addition to the actual packaging material, printing inks may give rise to taints, as may the action of container sealing, especially heat sealing of plastic containers.
- Local atmosphere. Some cases are known where taints have transferred from the local atmosphere to the food; for example, the odour from pesticide spraying. Other foods may cause transfer of taints; for example, onions stored in the same room as cakes are likely to impart a taint to the cakes.

Sensory analysis is an essential tool for investigating taint potential, as it can establish whether a taint problem is likely to develop; it can provide the first indication of a taint problem; or it can provide evidence to identify the nature of the taint and consequently potential hazard levels associated with it. It may require specialist procedures, as people vary in their sensitivity to different taints, and the sensory analyst may not necessarily be aware of the nature of the taint prior to setting up the test. It should also be borne in mind that interpretation of sensory tests based on normal statistical probabilities may not be the most appropriate. For example, the result of a difference test may report 'no statistically significant flavour difference between the control and test sample', even though a single assessor from the panel consistently and confidently described a taint in one of the products. Should the assessor's sensitivity be reflected in the consuming population for that product, then clearly his or her opinion is highly important. Using sensory analysis in this case as a screening or preventive method is therefore vital, as tainted products will result in loss of consumer confidence, waste valuable resources and, if they are proved to be potential hazards, the strong likelihood of criminal prosecution of the manufacturer.

Typical questions

- Is there a detectable difference in flavour/odour from the standard?
- How is the flavour/odour (taint) described? Is it detected immediately or in the after-taste?
- How many people detect this particular flavour/odour (taint)?
- How strong is the flavour/odour (taint)?
- How much does the flavour/odour (taint) affect the acceptability of the product?

1.8 Product acceptability

Successful food companies sell products and increase their profitability; unsuccessful companies do not! Of prime importance to food manufacturers is to design and market products that their customers want. Understanding the requirements of consumers in terms of production and processing variables is an essential application of sensory analysis in product development and marketing (case history, Chapter 10). It is important that knowledge about sensory characteristics is related to consumer likes or dislikes about the product. This is achieved through the proper design of appropriate tests as discussed in the guidelines and as illustrated in the case histories.

Typical questions

- Which product is preferred?
- How much is the product liked?
- Which product is most liked?
- How much is the appearance/flavour/texture liked or disliked?
- How much can products be changed before liking is affected?

How to use **2** sensory analysis to meet your objective

2.1.1 What is the question to be answered?

What is the purpose of the sensory test?

The purpose, or objective, of the sensory test should be explored and defined, and the feasibility of success determined, before any work is undertaken. Questions which should be asked to define the objective are discussed in Chapter 1. It is most important that the test selected will answer the question being asked and that the user recognizes the limitations of the test. For example, small samples sipped under controlled conditions will not answer questions related to the use of the product in a family meal.

The questions asked in the test objectives will often be answered by one or a combination of the tests classified by three main headings; difference tests, descriptive tests and acceptance tests.

2.1.2 What are the client's requirements?

Understanding the client's need

In all cases, it is important to know what the client expects and wants to get out of sensory analysis. A client is the person or company who requests or contracts the sensory test to be carried out. In many cases, the sensory project may stand alone, but it is more likely to form part of a larger project. The overall objectives of the client's project may well determine the specific objective of the sensory problem.

The way in which the data are to be linked with other information from the project must be considered to ensure that the separate objectives fulfil the overall objective of the project.

Specific problems may be associated with sensory analysis, and these need to be elicited before the experiment is designed. For example, assessment of meat treated in different ways will be influenced by within and between animal variation. Sample availability should be considered, as this may require a compromise in the methodology implemented.

Cost and time

Whether the client is internal (a colleague within a company) or external (another company), cost and time to achieve a result will be an important factor. The design of the test will need to be balanced against budget and resource in terms of availability of staff and facilities.

**2.2
Collection
of data**

In all cases, the questions asked should be clear, concise and with sufficient instruction for the participant in the test.

As the data generated are likely to require some form of statistical analysis, the questionnaire should be designed with the subsequent transfer of information to the computer in mind. For example, sufficient identification of assessor, sample and other necessary information should be recorded on each sheet to prevent possible mix-up of information at a future date. The scaling method should be considered in the light of the test objective and data analysis.

There are four basic types of scaling method commonly referred to: nominal, ordinal, interval and ratio. It is important that the sensory analyst understands the meaning of these, as this will affect the nature of the data obtained, and consequently the analyses used to make statements about the data.

A *nominal scale* is one where data are categorized by a name or number which acts as a label. Each observation collected must fall within one of the categories. For example, gender can be described by two categories M (male) and F (female). The categories have no logical ordering, and hence putting F before M would not affect the results.

An *ordinal scale* is one which allows observations to be ordered according to whether they have more or less of a particular attribute. Such scales are represented by numbers, where the lowest number usually denotes 'less of' and the highest number denotes 'more of'. Ordinal scales do not allow quantification of the amount of difference between observations. For example, the nine-point hedonic scale is ordinal, as is ranked data.

An *interval scale* is one where the distances or intervals between points on the scale are assumed to be equal. For example, if the perceptual distance between 1 and 2 on the hedonic scale was the same perceptual distance as between 2 and 3, 3 and 4, and so on, then this scale would have interval properties.

A *ratio scale* is one on which numbers can be expressed as ratios of each other. For example, 2 g is twice as heavy as 1 g, 6 m is three times as long as 2 m. An example of a ratio scale in sensory analysis is magnitude estimation. The main difference between interval and ratio scales is that the latter has a true zero, whereas the zero point of an interval scale is arbitrary.

Examples of some scales often used in sensory analysis are given in Figure 1.

Are the data to be collected by computer?

The computer should be as 'invisible' as possible, and the questionnaire format as near as possible to that of paper and pencil. Several computer based data-registration systems (systems which interact directly with the assessor) have been developed specifically for sensory analysis with the requirements of good sensory practices inherent in their design. Computer systems do not improve the results from sensory tests; this can only be effected by test design and panel use. Computer systems will improve the efficiency of sensory tests by providing the panel leader and the client with more rapid information on test results and on panel performance. There will also be an elimination of error in the data transfer which may be experienced in transferring data from paper to computer.

Numeric/integer (ordinal)

Not sweet   Very sweet

0	1	2	3	4	5	6	7	8	9

Boxes-Verbal (ordinal)

Not sweet   Very sweet

Not sweet	Slightly sweet	Moderately sweet	Very sweet	Extremely sweet

Line (ordinal or interval)

Not   Very

Magnitude estimation (ratio)

Please taste the reference sample (R) and allocate it a value of 100 to represent the sweetness intensity perceived.

Please taste each of the three samples in the order indicated. You are required to allocate each sample a number (not zero) indicating the degree to which it is more or less sweet than the reference sample.

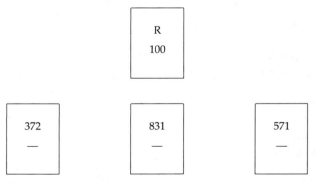

Figure 1   Examples of scales used in sensory analysis.

Analysis and future use of the data

The statistical tools used to analyse the data will depend on the nature of the test, and the type of analysis tool will determine the type and nature of the information derived from the data.

Often, data will be used at a future date to make a link with information collected by another source. An example is the linking of sensory-profile data with consumer acceptability data (e.g. preference mapping, section 5.2.6), chemical data or other physical measurements related to the samples.

To maximize the information obtainable from sensory data, collaboration with other departments is essential before proceeding with the sensory tests. Lack of communication at this stage will invariably cost money.

2.3.1 Discrimination or difference tests

What are discrimination or difference tests?

Discrimination or difference testing is used to determine whether there is a perceptible difference, or are differences, between two or more products and, in some cases, the magnitude of the difference. As these tests involve comparative judgements, they can be very sensitive in determining small differences between products.

What are the types of difference test?

Some tests are used to establish simply whether or not there is a difference between two samples. Such tests should not be used if there is an obvious difference between two products.

There are many types of difference test (Meilgaard *et al.*, 1987): the paired comparison test, the triangular test and duo trio test are among the most commonly used.

If the size of difference between samples is required then a rating scale will be required to make this measurement.

In the event of many samples being evaluated against a

control, then a multiple-difference test should be used (Meilgaard *et al.*, 1987). Multiple difference tests are used to measure the similarity or dissimilarity between the two samples in a pair, for all possible paired combinations of the samples in the test.

Which tests should be used in particular situations?

Paired comparison (difference) test

This test is used to determine if two samples differ in a specific character (BS 5929: Part 2, 1982). It is a directional test with a named attribute. For example, the assessor is presented with two samples and asked which sample is harder, or which sample is more bitter.

Taste order should be specified, and the test designed to ensure both possible orders are tasted an equal number of times. Samples should be presented under code, preferably with each assessor having unique codes to minimize accidental or deliberate influence of one assessor on another. The panel size should be a minimum of 20 members (see Section 4.3). Test result is determined by reference to a table of one-tailed paired-difference test (O'Mahony, 1986; Appendix Table A1).

Triangular test

This test is used to determine an unspecified sensory difference between two treatments (BS 5929: Part 3, 1984). The assessor is presented with three samples, advised that one may be different, and asked to identify which is the different sample.

Taste order is specified. Two presentations are possible: two Xs and one Y or two Ys and one X. Within each presentation three orders are possible, with the single sample tasted first, second or third, giving a total of six orders: YXX, XYX, XXY, XYY, YXY and YYX. Each order should be used an equal number of times; therefore the total number of assessors taking part in the test should be divisible by six.

Samples should be presented under code, preferably with each assessor having unique coding to minimize accidental or deliberate influence of one assessor on another.

If retrospective analysis is carried out (i.e. after the test) a panel of 24 assessors is recommended and test result determined by reference to standard tables (Appendix Table A2), by calculation to formula (O'Mahony, 1986), or by using a computer program such as MINITAB (1990).

There are two approaches to data collection available to the sensory analyst conducting a triangular test (BS 5926: Part 3, 1984). The first approach is known as the *forced-choice option*, where the assessor must choose an 'odd' sample. Using this approach, to determine whether there is a statistically significant perceivable difference between the samples, the sensory analyst simply counts up the number of correct responses and consults the appropriate tables (Appendix).

In the second approach, the sensory analyst allows the *no-perceivable-difference option*, and hence if the assessor genuinely cannot perceive a difference he/she can say so. With a panel trained in the use of difference testing, this is the better approach since the assessors should be allowed to express their findings as fully as possible. However in some instances, for example with consumers, the no-difference option may be seen as an 'easy' option and should be avoided.

In terms of data analysis, the no-difference option presents a problem, as the original 1/3 chance of choosing the odd sample no longer exists. To overcome this, many users add 1/3 of the no-difference responses to the correct responses and then consult the tables. Alternatively, the no–difference results can be discarded and only the results from those assessors who made a definite choice considered for analysis using the triangular test tables. However, it is important to remember that, particularly with a trained panel, the no–difference results provide you with important information about the nature of the samples.

If sequential analysis is carried out, as each assessor completes the test the panel, cumulative score is plotted until the accept or reject line is crossed (BS 5929; Part 3, 1984).

Duo-trio test

This test is used to measure unspecified differences between samples (BS 5929: Part 1, 1986). The assessor is presented with one sample (say A) and then a pair of samples (A and B) and asked to identify which of the pair matches the first sample. The statistical chance of obtaining the correct answer by guessing is the same as that of the paired difference test. Analysis of results is as for a one-tailed paired test above.

Two-out-of-five test

Multiple-sample tests can be used to determine the difference between two treatments (BS 5929: Part 1, 1986). In this test, the number of presentations is increased to five, (AABBB), and the assessor is instructed to identify the samples which are similar. The probability of chance discrimination is low (10%). Fatigue can be a problem but, where this is less so, as in colour or appearance work, a smaller number of assessors can be used to test for difference: eight to ten assessors, for example.

The results of the assessment can be checked against standard tables (BS 5929: Part 1, 1986), chi–squared or binomial distributions.

Ranking test

A ranking test with a specified attribute is used to establish a magnitude of difference between samples (BS 5929: Part 6, 1989). The assessors are presented with three or more coded samples and asked to rank them in order according to a single specific attribute, e.g. hardness, sweetness. The taste order should be prescribed and a balanced design used. Five samples is a reasonable upper limit and at least 30 assessors should be used. A variety of statistical tests are available to analyse the data, such as the Friedman rank test (O'Mahony, 1986).

Difference from control test

In this test the assessor is presented with an identified standard or control (Meilgaard *et al.*, 1987). Subsequent samples are rated on a scale indicating the degree of difference from the control sample, ranging from 'not different' to 'extremely different'. It is usual to include a hidden control. Assessors are also asked to indicate in what respect they consider the sample different. The data can be analysed using analysis of variance.

Magnitude estimation

Two or more samples are presented under code with a specified taste order which is balanced across assessors (Moskowitz, 1983). An arbitrary value for the attribute in question is assigned to the first sample. When the next sample is tasted a higher or lower value is assigned by the assessors according to their estimate of the magnitude of the difference. While this test is generally used to estimate differences in a specified characteristic, it can be used for acceptability or hedonic studies.

The first step in the data analysis is to convert the individual judgements to a common scale. This is achieved by modulus normalization (Moskowitz, 1977). Analysis can be by analysis of variance.

A difference test may not be appropriate for some products, where a long carry-over effect is known to exist, or where the sample has to be left in the mouth for some time (e.g. chewing gum). In all difference tests, a section of the form for recording comments should be available since this provides feedback on the reasons for the response.

What sort of panel is required?

A trained, untrained or consumer panel can be used to determine if there is a detectable difference between two or more samples. The size of the panel will depend on the difference test to be used, and the type of panel used. An untrained panel is not as sensitive to small differences as a trained panel, and therefore the size of an untrained panel should be much larger than a trained panel.

A consumer panel is rarely used for difference testing, due to the large numbers required for such an exercise. This task is often controlled by the marketing department within a company or commissioned with a market research agency. It can generally be assumed that if a trained panel cannot detect a difference between samples, then it is unlikely that an untrained or consumer panel will.

2.3.2 Descriptive tests

What are descriptive tests?

Descriptive tests are used to describe the sensory characteristics of a product, and to use these characteristics to quantify differences between products. Rating the descriptors for the sensory characteristics of appearance, odour, flavour, texture and after-taste will generate what is often referred to as the *sensory profile* of the product.

What are the types of descriptive test?

Free description, where assessors describe the sensory characteristics of a product, is a purely descriptive test. Some sensory analysts may obtain limited quantitative information using this method by counting the frequency with which particular attributes are used by the assessors, and this may be known as a limited or exploratory profile.

There are three main types of descriptive test where both qualitative and quantitative information are integral to the method. These are consensus profiling, conventional profiling (quantitative descriptive analysis–QDA) and free-choice profiling.

Which test should be used in particular situations?

Consensus profiling

This is a sophisticated descriptive technique developed by Arthur D. Little Inc. in 1948 (Cairncross and Sjostrom, 1950). Consensus profiling is carried out by a panel of four to six assessors who have been carefully selected and who have received lengthy training. The panel defines the character ratings of odour, flavour, taste and feeling factors, in terms of reference materials, and assigns ratings reflecting strength of note in the product. The order of occurrence of these odour and flavour ratings are recorded, as is the after-taste, one minute after swallowing. The panel also rates the overall degree of blend and amount of fullness present in the odour and flavour as a whole: this is called amplitude.

Several sessions are required to complete a profile. In the first session, general descriptions of overall impressions and characteristics are covered. Subsequent sessions are used to achieve a consensus on the odour and flavour character ratings, their intensities and order of appearance. To achieve a clear description, extensive use is made of reference materials. The panel members work together to achieve agreed standards.

Conventional profiling (QDA)

Conventional profiling is a term which is widely used in the UK to differentiate this type of profiling from free-choice and consensus profiling. Conventional profiling encompasses techniques which have been based on quantitative descriptive analysis (QDA), a profiling method developed by Stone *et al.* (1974) and marketed by the Tragon Corporation in the USA. Following its introduction in 1974, QDA found wide acceptance as the standard profiling method by many sensory analysts, who have adapted and modified the published technique to suit their own particular requirements.

While the terms 'conventional profiling' and QDA are often used synonymously in the UK, to avoid any unintentional confusion with the published Tragon method, the term 'conventional profiling' has been used throughout these guidelines. In this technique the number of assessors is often larger than in consensus profiling, usually six to ten. The criteria of selection are usually similar and the assessors are trained and experienced. Many organizations find that the time demands, coupled with the required calibre of the assessor, are such that part-time outside staff are recruited to carry out profiling.

In conventional profiling the preliminary stage is the collection of descriptors for appearance, odour, flavour, texture, mouth-feel factors and after-taste. All assessors contribute to the generation of descriptive terms. In the next stage these descriptors are organized by the panel leader, perhaps in consultation with the client, and an agreed rating sheet is drawn up. This is then presented to the panel for further refinement, accurate definition of terms and scale anchor points and presentation of standards. Finally, the samples are rated the appropriate number of times for the test design and these data are available for statistical analysis.

Most descriptors are rated on a continuous line scale with anchor points at each end. To minimize confusion, the scale is always organized so that the characteristic being measured increases in intensity from left to right. The sets of descriptors are tailored to each particular product test and may cover all sensory aspects or be restricted to, say, a flavour profile or a texture profile.

Basic rules for this work include coding all samples to reduce biases (section 6.3). If more than one sample is to be assessed, it is necessary to predetermine the order of assessment to ensure that all possible combinations of samples are presented an equal number of times. This may be changed if every assessor has to taste a control sample with a specified rating for an attribute before rating test samples.

Free-choice profiling

This technique has gained increasing acceptance in the UK since it was first reported in 1984, although many users have modified the original published method to make it more applicable to their particular use. In free-choice profiling (Williams and Langron, 1984) the need for carefully selected and highly trained assessors is less stringent. Assessors rate the samples on individually conceived terms and scales. The assessments are usually replicated and the test employs six to ten assessors. As with conventional profiling, the test can be structured to cover all sensory aspects, or be restricted to a profile on, say, flavour or texture.

Sophisticated multivariate statistical techniques (generalized Procrustes analysis) are used to construct multidimensional maps which identify descriptors that commonly discriminate between and describe the samples (McEwan and Hallett, 1990). As with conventional profiling, precautions are necessary to avoid biases, such as coding and balanced taste order.

What sort of panel is required?

A *trained panel* is the most usual type for conducting descriptive testing. This is because a trained panel is more capable of describing the subtle differences between samples. A trained panel is the only one recommended for the application of conventional profiling.

An *untrained panel* can be used for descriptive testing, although untrained assessors tend to be less sensitive to small differences. The technique of free-choice profiling is suitable for use with untrained panels, but may be more effective if the panel has received some basic training.

A *consumer panel* can be used for descriptive testing, but consumers do not readily describe what they perceive in detail. There are techniques, however, which can be used to elicit such information from consumers (Fransella and Bannister, 1977), for example using focus groups, but this is normally outside the role of the industrial sensory analyst.

2.3.3 Acceptance tests

What are acceptance tests?

Acceptance tests are used to evaluate product acceptability or to determine whether one or more products are more acceptable than others.

Acceptance testing should be applied using consumers, and because of this, acceptance testing is often seen as a market research function within a company. However, the sensory analyst can apply acceptance tests in a limited way to obtain an indication about product acceptability. In designing acceptance tests, it should be remembered that acceptability and preference are not the same thing. For example, a person may prefer one sample to another sample, but find them both unacceptable.

There are three main types of acceptance test presentations: monadic, paired and sequential monadic.

- In *monadic tests*, samples are presented one at a time.
- In *paired tests*, samples are presented two at a time.
- In *sequential monadic tests*, samples are presented in sequence to be assessed one at a time.

There are a number of different methods and scales used to determine and/or measure acceptance, including rank tests, paired preference tests, hedonic scaling and magnitude estimation.

Which test should be used in particular situations?

Paired comparison (preference) test

In this test the assessor is presented with two coded samples to establish whether there is a preference between the samples (BS 5929: Part 2, 1982). The test order given should ensure that each sample is assessed first and second an equal number of times. Both directions are of equal interest (two-tailed) as it is not known in advance which sample is preferred.

The panel size should be at least 50 (section 4.3). If the panel is drawn from staff on site, care should be taken to exclude people who may have particular knowledge of the nature of the work, or knowledge of the objectives for carrying out the work.

At the simplest level the assessor is asked to state which sample is preferred and reasons for preference. No-preference decisions are usually allowed and, although they are excluded from analysis, they are usually reported. Basic analysis is by reference to two-tailed binomial tables, and reasons for preference are tabulated. To give some measure of consistency of preference, assessors may be asked to make a preference judgement between two samples on one occasion and then to repeat the test on a second occasion, ideally 24 hours later.

There are four possible outcomes to this test; prefer A on both occasions (AA); prefer B on both occasions (BB); prefer A on the first occasion and B on the second occasion (AB); prefer B on the first occasion and A on the second (BA). Counting the number of consumers falling into each of these four cells, a two by two contingency table is created. A chi-squared test is then performed to analyse the data.

Multi-sample ranking for preference

This is a form of the ranking test (BS 5929: Part 6, 1989) except that the specified attribute is preference. Analysis is also by the Friedman rank test. Panel size should be at least 50 (section 4.3) and the panel should be drawn from people who have no particular knowledge of the nature of the work.

Hedonic rating

In this test the assessor is asked to indicate the extent of liking for the product from extreme dislike to extreme like. A full discussion of the choices of words and number of steps is given in Amerine *et al.* (1965).

A popular scale is the nine-point hedonic scale (Peryam and Pilgrim, 1957):

Like extremely
Like very much
Like moderately
Like slightly
Neither like or dislike
Dislike slightly
Dislike moderately

Dislike very much
Dislike extremely

In the analysis, each descriptor is assigned a value and it is usually assumed that it is an equal interval scale. An alternative approach is to score on a continuous line scale with the extremes at either end. The distance of the mark along the line is then used as a rating.

What sort of panel is required?

Under no circumstances should a trained panel be used to evaluate the acceptability of a sample. This is because such a panel will have been trained to evaluate samples objectively, and acceptability in this context is subjective.

An untrained panel (at least 50 people) can be used to evaluate the acceptability of a sample, or a range of samples. This would be the usual panel to use 'in house' (section 4.2.5). An untrained panel, however, will not normally represent the consuming public, and hence should only be used for an indication of acceptability.

Consumers can be used to evaluate the acceptability of a sample or range of samples, and are the best group to use. Market-place testing involving large numbers of people is normally considered outside the direct remit of the sensory function within a company. However, discussions between sensory analysts and marketing personnel, who normally contract such tests, must be actively encouraged to ensure correct experimental design and planning of associated sensory tests. If it is intended to use consumers, one should always follow the relevant codes of practice or guidelines, such as those contained in the Code of Conduct issued by the Market Research Society (1988).

The purpose of a questionnaire is to gather information. Most data for sensory analysis are collected through the use of a questionnaire, whether it is on paper or computer-generated. Correct design of the questionnaire is therefore important to ensure that all the necessary information is collected in a form in which it can be easily used. Data analysis must, therefore, be considered at the planning stages. Standard designs for certain questionnaires exist

**2.4
Principles of
questionnaire
design**

(e.g. hedonic forms, forms for triangle tests), and standardized questions for use in consumer studies are published by the Market Research Society (Wolfe, 1984). However, there are some general principles which can help in the design of questionnaires.

Examples of questionnaires for trained panels are available in many printed texts on sensory analysis (BS 5929 Parts 2–6; Stone and Sidel, 1985; Meilgaard *et al.*, 1987). Most contain some type of measurement scale which, together with the nature of the questions asked, have been developed over many years. Questionnaires for trained panels differ from those for consumer panels in that they do not generally require such detailed instructions, as familiarization with the test is an important part of training. Most of the remainder of this section gives examples which apply to the design of forms for acceptance or consumer tests and therefore those taking part are referred to as respondents rather than assessors. The principles, however, are also highly relevant to designing forms for trained assessors. In designing all forms it is important to consider how the data will be analysed and ensure that the information can be easily retrieved from the forms.

Where is the questionnaire to be used?

It is necessary to identify the target population: for instance, whether the participants will be part of a trained panel, selected from people 'on site', at home or in the street. The answer to this will determine the amount of detail, the type of questionnaire designed and whether it will be a self-completion questionnaire or one completed by an interviewer according to the responses given.

What type of question?

Questions can be broadly divided into closed-response or open-ended questions.

Closed-response questions ask for responses which fit into a category, and the respondent is often presented with a number of alternatives from which to choose, such as a nine-point hedonic scale or a scale designed to determine the frequency of purchase.

If multi-choice questions are used, it is necessary to

ensure that all alternatives are covered, or to use an 'other' option if not all alternatives can be practically included. Closed-response questions are easier to answer, tabulate and analyse as only a certain number of responses can be chosen. They are limited, however, in the amount of information they provide from a respondent. To give an example, Sample 609 may be preferred to Sample 538, but unless an open-ended question such as 'What did you prefer about Sample 609?' is included, the reason may not be apparent. If an interviewer is administering the ques-tionnaire, the respondent can be prompted to give a full response as follows:

Respondent:	'It's nicer.'
Interviewer:	'In what way is it nicer?'
Respondent:	'It tastes more like fresh orange juice.'
Interviewer:	'Is there anything else you can say about the sample?'
Respondent:	'No.'

It is important that the interviewer does not influence the answer by leading the respondent. For example:

Respondent:	'It's nicer.'
Interviewer:	'Do you think it is like fresh orange juice?'
Respondent:	'Well, yes, I suppose so.'
Interviewer:	'You don't want to say anything else, do you?'
Respondent:	'No, I don't think so.'

Open-ended questions give respondents the opportunity to express their opinion without the restraint of pre-specified categories. Open-ended questions are, however, more time-consuming to answer and the results are obviously far more difficult to analyse. This type of questioning may also be affected by bias from the way an interviewer asks the questions, by the limitations of the vocabulary of the respondent, and by bias by the reviewer in summarizing and reporting the results. It is, therefore, advisable to close as many questions as possible.

Questions should not place too much strain on the memories of respondents as the answers given may not be very precise. Where detailed information is required on a particular topic it may be necessary to record behaviour directly, through such means as diary records (Passmore and Eastwood, 1986).

How long should the questionnaire be?

The plan, structure and length of a questionnaire must encourage the respondent and keep his/her interest. The actual length will depend upon the number of questions that need to be asked, and on the place where the questionnaire is being completed. More questions can generally be answered when the respondent is in his/her own home than if he/she is stopped in the street. Where questionnaires are too long the respondent may become bored and the quality of response will be affected.

How should the questions be ordered?

The order of questions is particularly important when questioning untrained people or consumers. An introduction to the survey, without giving any information which may bias the answers given, is important to gain the initial co-operation of the respondents. The first question should be easily answered to put the respondent at ease and build up his/her confidence. Subsequent questions should lead the respondent logically through the topics, each topic being explored before progression to the next. Questions related to overall like/dislike should be asked first to avoid potential bias on subsequent questions in the interview. Sudden changes in topic should be avoided as they tend to confuse respondents and lead to indecision. Important questions are best asked near the beginning of the questionnaire when the respondent is most attentive and likely to give a more complete answer. Questions of a sensitive nature and general demographic classification questions are generally left until the end of the questionnaire, when the respondent is more at ease and has developed some trust in the interviewer and survey.

Questions for the main part of the questionnaire must be organized in such a way that a preceding question does not suggest the answer to subsequent questions. For instance, if you ask consumers how much they pay for orange juice and then ask them why they purchase that particular brand, price is likely to be mentioned as an important reason.

How should the questions be worded?

All questions should be written simply, using words that will be readily understood by the respondent. Technical phrases or specialized terms, unless they are commonly used by those taking part in the survey, should be avoided. Short questions are often easier to understand. The respondent is likely to become confused listening to long questions and may forget the points made at the beginning.

Questions need to be specific so that the respondent is clear about what sort of answer is required. For example. 'Do you often drink orange juice?' could produce a number of conflicting responses and would be clearer if it was written as two different questions as follows. 'Do you drink orange juice?' If the answer to this question is 'yes' you can then ask the second question: 'How often do you drink orange juice?' The answers can be categorized by actual times such as 'every day', 'at least once a week' and so on, rather than 'frequently', 'often', 'occasionally' etc.

Similarly, double-barrelled questions should also be avoided, such as 'What is your opinion of the flavour and texture of this sample?' The assessor may like the flavour, but dislike the texture. This could easily be separated into two questions.

Ambiguous words must be avoided or clarified. For example, to some people 'dinner' will mean a midday meal, and to others it will mean the meal they eat in the evening. Similarly, questions must not suggest an answer. For example, many respondents would probably agree with the statement 'you found that sample sweet, didn't you?', as it is easier to agree than to disagree. If asked 'what did you notice about the sample?', then it is likely that a smaller proportion of respondents would mention sweetness.

What should the final questionnaire look like?

If it is to be filled in directly by the respondent, then the questionnaire must look neat, easy to complete, with clear instructions and not overcrowded. The quality of reproduction is most important as the questions must be easy to read and not left open to interpretation due to poor photocopying or printing. If the questionnaire is to be filled in by an interviewer then the above points are important, but in addition the interviewer must be clear on the differentiation between instructions for them, and questions to ask. It is usual for interviewer's instructions to be printed in capitals to clarify this. The interviewer needs to be familiar with the layout of the questionnaire so that the respondent is encouraged by the fact that the interviewer knows what he/ she is doing.

It is often a good idea to pilot test a questionnaire to highlight any possible problems with the questions and also to make sure that the data can easily be analysed. A means by which the assessor and interviewer can be identified on a questionnaire will assist in cases where it is necessary to contact them for clarification of any points.

What samples are **3** being analysed?

Pre-testing with the use of pilot samples may be needed to answer some of the following questions depending upon knowledge and experience.

3.1.1 What are the products to be assessed?

Are the products comparable? Is there a set of samples which will answer the objectives?

It is not only prudent, but essential, to consider this question before embarking on any further planning or production/collection of samples. Will the factors to be measured be the dominant factors in the product? If factors which are irrelevant to the investigation cannot be held constant, then the results will not answer the objectives fully. Differences or preferences may be reported, but these will not necessarily be driven by the factors under study.

Are they safe?

It must be considered whether products are safe to consume or inhale. Factors which may affect the safety of products to the participants in sensory tests include microbiological status, chemical or toxic residues and ingredients which cause allergic responses or other health hazards.

It is a primary responsibility of those carrying out sensory analysis tests to ensure that assessors are not exposed to unacceptable risk as a result of participating in the tests.

The sensory analyst should also be aware of any statutory regulations which exist with respect to the control of substances which are considered hazardous to health, such as the UK Control of Substances Hazardous to Health (COSHH) Regulations 1988 (HMSO, 1988). This aspect is particularly important if the purpose of the analysis is to test for taint.

Are they palatable?

It may be necessary to prepare some samples into a more palatable form before proceeding with sensory analysis. For example, milk powder would be more palatable if re-constituted with water. It may be necessary to reduce the number of samples to be assessed if they are not very palatable.

What kind of production or preparation is needed?

It is important to ensure that all samples are produced or prepared in the same manner to enable true comparisons to be made between samples. Factors to consider include method of cooking, whether the samples need formulating into products, and the serving temperature.

Is the sample relevant to the objective?

Clearly the samples examined and the design of the test must answer specific questions posed by one or more of the objectives. It is essential to ensure that unwanted variables have been controlled or eliminated in the production of the samples.

In what context is the product eaten in this test?

Is it part of a meal? If so, consider practicalities such as sample preparation and experimental design.

Is it tested in a different physical state from that which is eaten in the finished product? If so, consider how the results can be related to the finished product.

Is all or part of the product to be evaluated? It is sometimes necessary to evaluate semi-processed parts of the final product as opposed to individual raw materials. For example, detailed data on intermediate products (cocoa butter, coffee extract etc.) would lead to increased knowledge of the process or formulation. If sensory tests are undertaken on such products, one must be clear about the reasons for doing this, and understand the consequences in terms of drawing conclusions on the final product.

3.1.2 Are there any special practical difficulties?

Consideration must be given to any aspect of the analysis that may cause difficulties for the perception of the assessor or panel. This includes order and session effects, strong flavours and odours, visual differences, temperature control of the product under test, and whether a carrier is needed.

Order and session effects

An *order effect* occurs when the perception of samples is influenced by the order in which they are presented. For example, a sensory characteristic in a second sample may be judged higher or lower than in the previous sample simply because of the effect of evaluating the first sample. If re-presented to the assessor the other way around, with the second sample presented first, the perception of this attribute would be different. Order effects cannot be eliminated in most sensory tests, but their impact can be substantially reduced by paying particular attention to experimental design and balanced presentations of samples across assessors and sessions.

A *session effect* occurs when the conditions of the test are altered in some way from session to session. As a simple example, if the temperature of the samples differs between sessions, and perceptions are affected by temperature (as would be the case of texture measurement in ice cream), session differences will tend to mask the real sample differences in any subsequent analysis.

Strong flavours and odours

Strong flavours and odours may mask characteristics which are being measured. For example, if the analysis of lemonade is carried out in a room which smells strongly of freshly brewed coffee, this will present difficulties for the assessors in determining the subtle flavour notes in lemonade. Also, strong odours on assessors themselves, such as oil, cigarette smoke, soap or perfumes, will make the sensory task much more difficult, not only for the assessor but also for the other members of the panel. Strong flavours and odours will also increase the fatigue rate amongst assessors and contribute heavily to carry-over effects. Order effects must, therefore, be taken into account in the design of the test. Sufficient time must be given between sample assessments, and palate cleansers should be used. The type of palate cleanser to use will vary according to the product under test and should be decided by the panel leader before the test. Suitable palate cleansers for use between samples will be bland in comparison to the product being tested, will have the effect of removing flavour/odour/residues of the previous sample, and should disappear quickly. Examples of palate cleansers which have been used successfully include mineral water, soda water, dilute lime juice, apple slices, natural yogurt (for curries and spices) and plain biscuits.

Visual differences

If specifically measuring flavour or texture, any visual differences should be masked to prevent bias. For example, in a difference test (section 2.3), assessors will be influenced by the appearance of products when making the judgement as to whether samples are different in flavour and texture. Masking of visual differences can often be achieved through the use of coloured lights or non-transparent cups with lids and straws.

Temperature control of the product under test

If the temperature of the samples at the time of the analysis varies from assessor to assessor, or from one replication to another, a non-relevant difference may be introduced into the results. In some cases, the temperature of the product will strongly influence the perception of the sensory attributes: for example, the texture characteristics of ice cream are very temperature dependent. Suitable facilities must be available to bring or maintain the product at the correct temperature and to hold it for the required length of time.

Is a carrier needed?

A suitable food medium can be used to dilute very strong flavours and odours, but it must be bland, non-interactive with the product to be tested, and create a matrix that represents a normal medium for the product type. In the analysis of strong sauces, such as soy sauce or Worcester-shire sauce, mashed potato or bread could be useful as a carrier product.

3.2.1 How many product types are there?

The samples presented for analysis may be different varieties of the same type of product (ie. several brands of soluble coffee) and/or different formulations of one product representing, for instance, different ingredient levels (ie. formulations of one brand of soluble coffee). It is necessary to establish the product types prior to considering the experimental design (Chapter 5).

3.2.2 Is it necessary to evaluate every product?

It is very likely that time and money can be saved by careful consideration of the sample set. For example, if the products fall into groups because of their nature, it may be possible to reduce the number of samples to be evaluated by using group representatives. The consequences of reducing the number of samples by elimination are referred to in more detail in section 5.1.2. In most cases, in order to meet the objectives of the area under investigation, it is necessary to retain the appropriate samples in the experimental design. For example, to reduce five samples increasing in sweetness concentration, to three samples, elimination of Samples 2 and 4 would still ensure retention of the original range of concentration.

3.2.3 How much sample is available?

In most circumstances, the panel leader will stipulate the amount required to fit the experimental design. Questions of replication, number of assessors, etc. will be considered in the experimental design and will therefore affect the amount required. In addition, certain test designs require a designated control sample to be assessed after or before each test sample (section 2.3) In such cases, it will be necessary to ensure that sufficient amounts of the reference are available for the duration of the test.

The way in which samples are packed and stored should also be considered. Samples supplied in bulk should be broken down into smaller units and stored for the duration of the test. This will eliminate factors such as 'settling' in bulk containers (resulting in unrepresentative samples) and risk of product loss (accidental damage or spillage). Non-bulk samples (e.g. jars of jam) may exhibit considerable within-sample variability (the fruit may be at the top of the jar). In this case, it would be necessary, therefore, to establish what constitutes a unit (e.g. one jar) and how many samples can be taken from each unit (one spoonful per jar).

It is always wise to remember that additional, representative samples are unlikely to be available after the start of the test and that sufficient product should be put aside to cover all eventualities.

3.3 Product assessment

3.3.1 How many products should be assessed in one sitting?

The actual number of products presented will depend on many factors, the most important of which are as follows:

The nature of the assessment

More products can be assessed within a session when visual or tactile analyses are made than if the product has to be tasted or evaluated for odour. This is because the taste and odour senses are more easily fatigued.

The nature of the product

Fewer products can be assessed if the products have strong flavours or odours, or if the after-tastes linger (section 3.1.2).

The number of questions asked about the sample

The total number of judgements asked of the assessor should not lead to boredom with a given task or sensory/ physical fatigue. Therefore, if a large number of questions are being asked about each sample, fewer samples should be given.

The amount of sample the assessor requires to do the analysis

This will depend on the test method and the number of judgements needed on each product. The number of judgements affects portion size, and therefore the amount of product needed for the test (section 3.2.3). In tasting, the more judgements asked of the assessor for a given product, the more samplings have to be made, and the more likely that this will lead to sensory fatigue.

The experience and training of the assessors

A motivated, trained and experienced assessor will be able to manage more tasks than a novice, as they will be more familiar with what is required of them and have wider knowledge of likely product characteristics. They will be able to make many judgements without having to sample products repeatedly, thus reducing sensory fatigue.

3.3.2 What are the practical limits for the number of products tested?

In preparing a product for the assessors, the practical limitations of the preparation and presentation facilities must be considered. A design which requires simultaneous presentation to nine assessors, for example, would be inappropriate if the facilities are unable to seat nine assessors, or if it is impossible to prepare sufficient sample for nine assessors at any one time. Consider all the constraints to determine the maximum number of samples which can be presented at any one time.

3.3.3 How is the product to be assessed?

The way in which the product should be assessed may or may not be stipulated in the instructions to the assessor. Allowing the assessor to evaluate products in his/her own way will introduce more variability to the panel's response.

In sensory tests designed for smaller numbers of assessors making precise judgements on well-defined attributes, it will be necessary to define exactly how to evaluate the attribute in the instructions to the assessor. With texture measurements, the orientation of the product in the mouth at analysis should be described: for example, 'initial hardness' is assessed by biting with the front teeth.

Who are the right 4 people for sensory analysis?

4.1.1 Sensory analyst or panel leader

For sensory analysis to be successful, it is necessary for someone to take the responsibility to ensure that tests are carried out in the correct and appropriate manner. This is the role of the sensory analyst or the panel leader. The sensory analyst requires formal training, usually as part of his or her further education, although someone who develops the responsibility for sensory analysis within a company, will often build up his or her knowledge based on practical experience.

The sensory analyst may, or may not, also act as the panel leader depending upon the size of the sensory department and the amount of work which it is required to do. The role of the panel leader is to ensure that the panel performs to the best of its ability and that the tasks set for the panel are effectively completed. In all cases, successful sensory analysts and panel leaders will possess certain common characteristics, and for companies looking to utilize sensory-testing procedures, it is important to bear these in mind when selecting an appropriate person. The individual should have an active interest in people, and be able to earn their respect. He or she should be able to lead without being dictatorial, should have an active interest in the product, an active interest in the work, and should be able to organize work, time and resources. He or she must be able to decide and advise on the correct procedure, to analyse and report on work and to integrate his/her work with that of other departments.

4.1.2 Sensory assessors

Many factors affect the ability and performance of assessors in sensory tests. Selecting and training appropriate assessors is a time-consuming but nonetheless essential part of planning any sensory test.

The requirements for assessors will ultimately depend upon the types of test being carried out, but the basic requirements for any person taking part in sensory analysis as an assessor are as follows:

Availability and willingness to participate

Assessors must be available to attend sessions when required. In industry, this may not only require the agreement of the person taking part in the test, but also the permission of the manager to whom they are responsible. The time commitment should be made quite clear as it is essential for preparation and planning that assessors arrive on time. For assessors taking part in long-term trials, the panel leader should be aware of planned holidays or other commitments which may affect assessors' availability.

It should be stressed that the successful use of sensory analysis in product development and quality control is dependent upon the availability of assessors when required. Unless there is a real commitment from senior management, the panel leader will always find this to be a major problem. In many companies, assessors are appointed on a part-time basis solely for this purpose, which confers many advantages in the training of individuals and the throughput of sensory tests.

In addition to being available, assessors should be interested, keen, enthusiastic and prepared, if necessary, to test 'different' or 'unusual' products, as would be the case if part-processed products have to be tested (section 3.1.1).

Ability to perform the task

After initial practical tests, a person should have shown the capability to follow instructions and to carry out the appropriate tests in the correct manner. Powers of concentration are an essential element and, at this stage, it is often possible to gain an indication of who is likely to become a competent assessor. Initial practical tests may also give an indication of reliability, in that the sensory results of individuals must be consistent both within a session and from session to session.

Health and personal habits

Some people may be allergic to certain test products, or constituents of these (e.g. milk, eggs or colourants), and should therefore be excluded from tests on these products. Also, if anyone is suffering from temporary ill health, such as colds, upset stomachs, or toothache, they should not be included on the sensory panel. Pregnancy may also affect taste perceptions, so it is generally advisable not to recruit pregnant women onto the panel.

If colour analysis is involved, people should have good colour discrimination, and should not be colour-blind. It is worth noting that colour-blindness, or deficiencies in discrimination between colours, is more prevalent in men than in women. Colour blindness is easily tested using the standard method described by Ishihara (1967).

As described in section 3.1.2, strong odours may influence the perception of certain sensory characteristics. Assessors should therefore be discouraged from using odorous cosmetics when attending panels, or from washing hands with perfumed soap. Assessors should also be discouraged from smoking or eating strong foods prior to testing, as they may not only influence their own perception but also that of others sitting close by. Soiled overalls, if contaminated with oil or grease, for example, should be removed before entering the tasting area.

Personality and seniority of assessors

Assessors may be required to be interactive within a group situation, for example when generating terms for descriptive analysis. It is important, therefore, that there are no dominating individuals within the group. Such a person may be either an individual with a domineering personality who would seek to impose their views on others, or a dominant individual within the company hierarchy. Junior staff may be less willing to express their true thoughts and ideas, and more willing to accept the ideas which come from senior staff on the panel. Equally, one should not recruit individuals with a very passive or indecisive personality, as they would be unlikely to express their opinion and contribute fully to group sessions, or may find it difficult to make firm decisions on product characteristics.

In certain situations, it may be difficult to control who takes part in sensory tests. This may be particularly true in industrial situations. In all cases, however, the basic principle to follow is to insist that assessors write down their comments, and only allow discussions after this has been completed by all assessors. Any conclusions drawn can then be based on written judgements which are less subject to influence or bias.

4.2
Selecting people for specific tasks

Many people are able to complete some form of sensory analysis successfully. However, people differ in their capabilities and it is frequently necessary to define the task and what is required as a preliminary to selection.

4.2.1 Quality control

Quality control involves routine checking to ensure that product quality is within the specified range, according to an agreed specification or other production criteria. In order to carry out effective quality control, assessors must have a depth of knowledge which can only be gained by long periods of practical testing or by intensive exposure to the product range and defects which are likely to occur. They must also be able to make allowances for normal within batch variation, or batch-to-batch variation. In addition, they should be exposed to training from a sensory analyst, so that they are aware of the basic principles of good sensory practice and, of course, to ensure that they have been screened to be suitable for the job. Particular attention should be focused on their ability to recognize the presence of off-flavours or taints. It is not unknown for a product to be passed by the quality control department, yet ultimately rejected by the consumer because of the presence of a taint.

4.2.2 Taint tests

If the purpose of the sensory test is to confirm or determine the nature of a suspected or unspecified taint, as would be the case in a consumer complaint, then it is wise to use as many assessors as possible, provided they are familiar with the test procedures. This would maximize the chance that some assessors will be sensitive to the taint. If the purpose of the sensory test is to establish the presence of a known taint, such as chlorophenols, assessors who have been screened for their sensitivity to chlorophenols should be used. Advice on screening assessors for sensitivity to taints is given in section 4.4.1.

4.2.3 Discrimination or difference tests

The initial panel-screening procedure should be planned with respect to the products which will be evaluated. For instance, if saccharin is a major component within products, it is important to know whether potential assessors can perceive it. A general familiarity with the food types to be tested is also advisable.

Assessors should be familiar with the format of the test, the task they are to carry out, and the analysis procedure (for example, whether to smell or taste, the mouth cleansing procedure etc.). The more complex the test, however, the greater the training time that will be required. Individuals who have been involved in the manufacture, development or preparation of the samples must not be used in these tests as they may be aware of the nature of the changes introduced into the product.

4.2.4 Descriptive tests

Assessors will need to be specifically selected using a range of the products to be assessed and they will need to have received specialist training before participating in the final test procedure. All the basic requirements listed in section 4.1 are of particular importance. In addition, assessors must have the ability to describe the perceived characteristics and discuss the definition of terms, be able to perceive the same (similar) characteristics in a variety of foods, must work well as a member of a team and must not be involved in the development or processing of the product under test.

4.2.5 Acceptance tests

Sensory analysts will normally have the responsibility for organizing 'in-house' preference or acceptability tests. The term 'in house' refers to tests carried out on company premises with company staff, and not in the homes of consumers. Suitable assessors will be any member of the staff who is likely to eat the product, provided they are not involved in any way with the product under test, or have been previously selected and trained for discrimination and descriptive tests.

In many companies, acceptance tests involving direct contact with the consumer are usually seen as the responsibility of the marketing department. A sensory analyst should play a part, however, and at least have the opportunity of discussing the objectives of the test, the questions to be asked and the nature of the target population with those carrying out tests.

**4.3
How many
assessors?**

The number of assessors required to carry out an analysis depends on a number of factors including the test procedure, the purpose of the test, the amount of assessor training, the reproducibility of their results and the variability of the product. The panel should be large enough to overcome such variability. If a panel is too small, the results are too dependent on individual judgements. However, smaller, highly trained, sensitive panels usually give more reliable results than larger, less trained and therefore less sensitive groups.

Another issue in relation to the number of assessors is that, in some circumstances, too many assessors combined with a sensitive test may in fact lead to a significant result. This is particularly true in difference testing, where increasing the number of assessors increases the chance of rejecting the null hypothesis. In such tests, it is well worthwhile looking at the β level as well as the α level, as discussed in section 5.2.7.

Several publications suggest numbers for different types of test. As a guide, these numbers are summarized in Table 1. The numbers for each test should be at least those quoted as these have been chosen to balance all risks. Not using this minimum number may increase the risk of wrong conclusions being drawn on the results of the sensory test. A pool of assessors at least 50% greater than the number required in testing should be maintained.

<table>
<tr><td>4.4.1 Selection on ability</td><td>**4.4
How to select
assessors**</td></tr>
</table>

Initial screening for general ability

Initial screening tests may include recognition and perception of primary tastes (ISO 3972, 1979). Primary tastes are sweet, salt, acid (sour) and bitter. Typical solutions to use for initial screening of assessors are as follows:

- sweet, 16 g/l sucrose
- salt, 3 g/l sodium chloride
- acid, 1 g/l citric acid
- bitter, 0.02 g/l quinine sulphate (or hydrochloride).

Similarly, initial screening tests may include recognition and definition of odours. This is best achieved through the presentation of odour bottles containing a small amount of chemical on cotton wool. Suitable chemicals depicting typical food-related odours or flavours can be obtained from companies specializing in the sale of food flavourings: e.g. citrus oil (orange or lemon), eugenol (cloves/dentists), hexanal (green), cedar oil (woody), 'smoke', 'condensed milk'.

Colour vision or tests for colour-blindness should be carried out using the tests proposed by Ishihara (1967).

Initial screening for ability to detect specific taints

If screening assessors for specific taints, such as chlorophenols or sulphur dioxide, a dilution series of the pure chemical should be prepared, either in water or in a bland oil if it is not water-soluble. The series should range from slightly below the known threshold concentration (ASTM, 1973) to

Table 1: Recommended minimum number of assessors for sensory tests

Difference test	
Paired test	
Assessors	30
Selected assessors	20
Triangular test	
Assessors	24
Selected assessors	18
Two-out-of-five test	
Selected assessors	12
Duo-trio test	
Assessors	32
Selected assessors	20
Ranking test	
Assessors	30
Rating test	
Assessors	20
Selected assessors	8
Descriptive test	
Selected assessors	8
Acceptance tests	
(Caution! refer to Section 2.2.3)	
Two-sample preference test	
Assessors	50
Multi-sample ranking for preference	
Assessors	50
Hedonic rating	
Assessors	70
Magnitude estimation	
Assessors	70

Note: 'Assessor' refers to a person carrying out the sensory test. 'Selected assessor' refers to assessors who have been selected because of their sensitivity and ability to perform the test in question.

about one hundred times this value. Individual assessors should be screened for their ability both to detect and to describe the odour of the compound. This can be done either by a series of difference tests against a control, or by an interrupted ascending series using hidden controls. In each test, assessors should be asked to describe the stimulus. Those assessors who identify the lower concentrations should be selected for taint tests.

Ability to perform test procedures

Ability to follow the sensory test procedure is the minimum criterion for all tests.

Ability to perform difference, rating and ranking tests can be assessed by varying the concentration of a constituent in foods, (e.g. salt in soup, citric acid in fruit drinks), and presenting the samples to the assessors as specific tests.

With descriptive tests, assessors may be given a number of samples of a product which are known to differ (for example different brands of chocolate or brands of soluble coffee), and be asked to describe the sensory characteristics of each. The number and type of the descriptions will indicate whether a particular individual is likely to make a good assessor for descriptive tests. It is also important that the descriptions generated are not subjective.

4.4.2 Measurement of ability

Ability and sensitivity will increase with training, so the criteria for selection should not be excessively harsh. It is suggested (Meilgaard *et al.*, 1987) that only candidates scoring more than 60% in an 'easy' or 40% in a 'moderately' difficult triangular test should be selected; in descriptive tests a candidate should use a relevant descriptor for 60% of samples and in a ranking test should only invert adjacent pairs.

4.5.1 General training

**4.5
How to train
assessors**

Training generates increased awareness, both of what is expected of the assessors and of their product knowledge.

The amount of training given to selected assessors is dependent on the type of analyses that they will be required to take part in. In all cases, this should initially be designed to encourage assessors and can be facilitated by immediate feedback of results after each session.

All assessors should be given training in how to use the senses and, if possible, some formal instruction or lectures on the sense organs. This will help them to understand the complexity of the tasks which will be asked of them. Examples of tests which can be used to train assessors in the use of the senses are well documented in Jellinek (1985).

All assessors should receive practical instruction on the test procedure (e.g. whether to spoon or sip, to spit or swallow), the format of the test (e.g. how the sensory laboratory works, familiarization with the booths, whether samples are presented singly or in sets, how to alert the experimenter, what to do after completing tests), the test forms or the use of the computer-based data registration system (e.g. how to follow the form, what has to be recorded, how to interact with the computer).

4.5.2 Training for specific tasks

Difference, rating and ranking tests

In order to investigate whether assessors are consistent, they should take part in a series of mock difference, ranking or rating tests on foods likely to be evaluated, in which the same samples are presented on more than one occasion. If a new test procedure is to be introduced which is unfamiliar to the panel, or if rating is required for an unfamiliar attribute, further training should be given.

Descriptive tests

Assessors need to be able to detect, describe and repeatedly quantify sensory characteristics of the food. In order to do this, they need to be exposed to a wide range of products under test in order to gain experience of the varying appearance, flavour and texture. For this reason, the panel leader should acquire both the product range and other samples illustrative of specific attributes for use before and during training. In addition, assessors should be encouraged at all times to describe a wide range of foods and chemicals to increase their awareness of the range of attributes likely to be encountered.

The training steps should be approached as follows:

1. *Use of intensity scales.* Assessors are familiarized with the use of the full range of a scale and tested on their ability to use a scale in a consistant manner. This can be achieved by presenting assessors with a known concentration of a substance in a food (for example adding sucrose to apple sauce).
2. *Word generation.* Assessors evaluate three or four different samples of a product, writing down as many terms as they can to describe the sensory characteristics fully.
3. *Discussions.* Assessors agree on what terms are relevant and either arrive at definitions for each term (BS 5098, 1975), or agree when terms should be used. At this stage it is frequently useful to have other products available which may help to explain a particular term to other panel members.
4. The word-generation and discussion stages need to be repeated on several occasions to enable the assessors to define and agree on the attributes over a range of the product. They should be encouraged to concentrate on a limited number of terms at each session.
5. A 'simple' profile is drawn up and tested by *replicate assessments* on a number of samples.
6. Feed-back to the panel and further discussions to rectify any problems.

Further, more detailed training will be necessary before conventional profiling (QDA) is undertaken.

Acceptance tests

Specific training is not required; however, assessors should be made familiar with the test procedure and be clear about the instructions given.

Experimental design **5** and data analysis

5.1.1 What is experimental design?

Experimental design, in the most general sense, is simply the correct planning and execution of a sensory test.

Experience and common sense are the two main components of designing an experiment to meet your objectives. For example, in a paired-comparison test, there are only two possible presentations (AB and BA), unless it is desired to test like with like, in which case there are four possible presentation orders: AB, BA, AA and BB. Designs for difference tests are well documented (Stone and Sidel, 1985; Meilgaard *et al.*, 1987).

Statistical experimental design is one important tool which sensory analysts should use to minimize sources of error and/or variation when collecting their data. This aspect of design also relies on experience, but initially reading a good textbook such as Stone and Sidel (1985), attending a course, or consulting an applied statistician will provide a good starting point.

Keep records of your experimental plans and designs as it is likely that they will be useful for the future.

5.1.2 What factors should be taken into account in the experimental design?

Is there help available from a statistician?

Most sensory analysts will have acquired a basic understanding of statistics. However, many will benefit from the advice of a statistician in the design and analysis of the most effective test. If a statistician is not available for consultation, it is recommended to refer to Stone and Sidel (1985) or Cochran and Cox (1957). The former reference is specific to sensory problems. Whether or not a statistician is available for advice, the following additional questions must be considered in experimental design of sensory tests.

How many assessors?

The number of assessors (section 4.3) will depend on the type of panel used, the type of test used, and preparation constraints.

How many samples are there?

This will depend on the object of the experiment: too few samples and information may be lost; too many samples and the experiment may become too costly. Sample availability must also be a consideration (section 3.2.3). The number of samples presented at any one session will depend on the type of panel and the nature of the product.

How many replicates are necessary?

In these guidelines, a replicate is defined as a repeated judgement on a sample by an assessor. The number of replicate judgements will depend on the type of test. In difference tests, a large panel is better than a small panel providing replicate judgements. With descriptive profiling, two replicates (i.e. three assessments per sample and assessor) are normally considered adequate. However, replication is expensive in time and resource, and industry often does not replicate, as a single assessment is often considered sufficient to achieve the objectives.

Nonetheless, before making the decision to reduce replication, the sensory analyst must be confident that the panel is consistent and reliable. If the panel is fully trained and constantly evaluating the same type of product, then a single assessment is likely to provide reliable data from descriptive analysis. However, if the panel is evaluating different products all the time, then replication is advisable. Although replication is recommended for acceptability tests, in practice, the need to present the samples to the same panel of assessors on several occasions will make acceptability tests expensive and impractical.

Suitable replication provides more confidence in results.

How will possible order effects be evaluated?

An order effect occurs when the observations of assessors
are influenced by the order in which they assess samples.
The order of presentation to each assessor should therefore
be designed to balance out potential order effects. If order
effects are thought to be likely, then the sample presentation should be designed to allow some measure of it to be
made and allowed for during the analysis. It would be
helpful in such instances to consult a statistician, or refer to
a useful text such as Stone and Sidel (1985). The effect of
order can be evaluated using analysis of variance (section
5.2).

How will a possible session effect be evaluated?

With some products, for example where serving temperature is important, a session effect may occur (i.e. the
temperature may vary from session to session). In such an
event the sample presentation should be designed to allow
some measure of this to be made and allowed for during the
analysis. Again it is advisable to consult a statistician or a
suitable text such as Stone and Sidel (1985). Session effects
can be evaluated using analysis of variance (section 5.2).

How will possible within-sample variation be evaluated?

With some products there is often large variation between
samples which are nominally the 'same'. When this is the
case, a measure of the within-sample variation should be
made (e.g. standard deviation), and taken into account
during the execution of the experiment and analysis of the
data.

When would more advanced design techniques be appropriate?

Factorial designs are appropriate if several treatments are
applied at different levels to a sample. This type of design is

particularly useful in new product development and product reformulation. However, it is not often practical to look at all combinations of sample formulation and therefore an incomplete design needs to be considered. These should be selected with care, with due consideration given to which treatments are of primary interest. Cochran and Cox (1957) is a good basic text, but consultation with a statistician will ensure that you get the most from your data.

How many samples should be tasted by each assessor?

The number of samples tasted by each assessor will depend on the total number of samples investigated and the information that is required from the experiment.

In descriptive profiling it is desirable for all samples to be evaluated by all assessors. This is essential when applying free-choice profiling, as the data-analysis procedure used requires complete data sets.

In acceptability studies it is often only possible to have a few of the samples evaluated by each assessor. If this is the case, a balanced incomplete block design (Stone and Sidel, 1985) is useful. However, if the acceptability data from each assessor are to be related individually to profile data, then each assessor must evaluate every sample. Also, complete data sets allow analysis of results from individuals, which is often useful for segmentation and performance purposes.

What is the size of difference to be detected?

Generally, the smaller the difference to be detected the more observations that are required to prove statistical significance. Remember, however, that the size of difference between samples is seldom known in advance.

Should there be a control sample?

A control sample is useful for product matching, monitoring changes in a sample over time, quality control purposes and as a measure of panel efficiency. Ideally the control should remain constant throughout the duration of the experiment, though this is sometimes difficult in practice, particularly with shelf-life projects.

Before starting to run endless statistical analyses, it is important to decide what is really required from the data. In making this decision, consider who the results are for (section 7.1), and the questions which are to be answered. In addition, examine the statistical resources available. The following are some questions which might be asked.

- Is it important to represent the data visually, using different graphical tools? What graphical capabilities are available?
- Should the data be summarized? Which summary statistics are most appropriate and can they be easily calculated? Are they being summarized in the correct way (e.g. by assessor, by attribute, by sample)?
- Is a particular hypothesis being tested: e.g. is the creaminess of a chocolate bar greater than the creaminess of another chocolate bar? Is it necessary to quantify the confidence associated with concluding that the two samples are different?
- Is it important to illustrate the relationship between six formulations of yoghurt and the 22 sensory attributes used to describe them, as a two- or three-dimensional picture? Is a statistical package with multivariate data analysis capabilities available?
- Is acceptability information to be related to sensory profile data? Is there access to the appropriate tools, and can they be used with confidence?

The following sections should help in answering some of these questions.

5.2.1 What statistical methods are available?

Exploratory visual methods

These are simple graphical procedures, such as histograms and line graphs, which can be used to examine the shape and trends present in the data. Most computer-based data-analysis packages include simple graphics as a standard feature.

Univariate methods

These are a collection of statistical procedures which consider one sensory attribute at a time: for example, comparing two samples for perceived sweetness, then comparing them for bitterness and so on.

Multivariate methods

These are a collection of statistical procedures which consider two or more sensory attributes simultaneously. For example, the interrelationships between all the described attributes in a profile are used to make statements about how samples differ from each other.

Parametric methods

These are a class of statistical methods which make the assumption that the data collected has an underlying normal distribution. These methods are powerful, and provide precise information about data, providing the assumptions hold. However, some methods are not robust to failures in assumptions. For further information refer to O'Mahony (1986).

Non-parametric methods.

These are a class of statistical methods, sometimes referred to as distribution free methods, which make limited assumptions about the data. In the case of sensory-related data the only assumption which may need to be satisfied is symmetry of the data. These methods are more robust than parametric methods, but provide less precise information. For further information refer to O'Mahony (1986).

5.2.2 How to decide if the data are normally distributed

This is not an easy task, since often it is not the actual raw data which need to follow this distribution, but the residual after performing the analysis. Residuals are the difference between the observed and the expected data, where the expected data are determined by the statistical method being used. For example, in analysis of variance it is the residual which needs to be normally distributed, but with a t-test it is the actual data which need to satisfy the assumptions.

A quick visual method is to plot a histogram of the raw or residual data and judge whether it has a symmetrical bell shape. It is not easy to conduct a formal test of normality, but a simple graphical procedure is available. This involves plotting the required data (raw or residual) against corresponding normal deviates (Neave, 1989). A straight line should result if the data satisfy normality. O'Mahony (1986) and a good basic book on statistics (e.g. Chatfield, 1983) are recommended for further reading. In addition a good statistics package will allow the normality assumption to be tested.

A general rule of thumb is that all consumer data should be analysed using the non-parametric methods mentioned in this section. Data collected from a trained sensory panel can be analysed using parametric methods, provided it has been established that the panel is well trained.

It is a good idea to analyse trained panel data using both parametric and non-parametric methods. If the same conclusion is consistently reached, then use the parametric methods. However, it is worthwhile to inspect data for strange observations and conclusions.

5.2.3 Which methods are appropriate for discrimination tests?

Which statistical method should be used?

The most commonly applied discrimination tests are based on the probability of a particular event occurring. For example, in a paired comparison test there is a 50% chance of a correct 'guess', while in a triangular test there is a 33.3% chance of a correct 'guess'. Pre-calculated tables are readily available to eliminate the need for manual calculations (Appendix).

Should a one-tailed or two-tailed test be used?

A *one-tailed test* is used if the direction of the response is known in advance. For example, if the question asked is 'Which sample is sweeter?' and the experimenter knows the correct answer, then a one-tailed (one-sided) test is used. In fact, triangular, duo-trio and paired comparison (difference) tests all use a one-tailed test.

A *two-tailed test* is used if the direction of the response is not known in advance (O'Mahony, 1986): for example, asking which of two samples is sweeter, but not knowing in advance which one is.

5.2.4 Which methods are appropriate for descriptive tests?

Simple visual representation

Graphical methods such as histograms, line graphs and spider diagrams (Chapter 9) are very useful. These will allow attribute differences between the samples to be observed.

Exploratory statistics

Means and medians provide a measure of the location or centre of the data. Standard deviations and interquartile ranges provide a central measure of spread in the data. Box and whisker diagrams can be used to represent these measures visually (Velleman and Hoaglin, 1981).

Confidence intervals

Calculate a confidence interval for the mean of each sample. This can be done for each attribute separately. A pooled confidence interval can be calculated across all attributes, provided that each attribute has the same standard deviation. As a word of caution, in comparing samples in a descriptive test for overlap on a particular attribute, one is, in effect, being conservative. In other words, the degree of overlap between samples is greater than would be expected had the two samples been directly compared.

Comparing two sample means

To compare directly whether two samples differ with respect to a particular attribute, then a two-sample t-test can be performed. This tests whether the means of the two samples are different. If the data for the two samples were obtained from the same assessors then a t-test for related data would be appropriate. In effect, this is the same as subtracting the data for the first sample from the second and testing whether the mean difference is different from zero. However, if different assessors were used to evaluate the two samples, then a t-test for unrelated data would be used.

Comparing more than two sample means

To test whether the means of more than two samples are different with respect to a particular attribute, then analysis of variance should be used. This is an extension of the t-test.

One-way analysis of variance

For each assessor a one-way analysis of variance could be performed to ensure that each member of the panel was using an attribute to distinguish between the samples. This is a good method of panel monitoring.

Two-way analysis of variance

Two-way analysis of variance can be performed where both sample and assessor variation are calculated. It is not unusual for an assessor effect to be present, as this tends to reflect differences in scale use.

Two-way analysis of variance with interaction

If replication was included in the data collection, then it is possible to measure the interaction between assessors and samples. There are two possible causes for the presence of an interaction effect. It may be due to differences in scale use by different assessors, but this tends not to be a problem. However, if the interaction is due to members of the panel in effect placing the samples in a different order on the scale, then this is serious as it means there has been a problem not observed during the training. This can be detected by examining or plotting the raw data (O'Mahony, 1986).

Where are the sample differences?

Analysis of variance may indicate that the sample means of more than two samples are different, but does not identify where these differences lie. To find this out there are a number of multiple comparison tests which can be used: e.g. Fisher's least significant difference, Scheffe, or Duncan's multiple-range test (O'Mahony, 1986).

Evaluating other sources of variation

Analysis of variance can be used to evaluate potential order effects, session effects and within sample variation. These effects are specified as sources of variation in the same way as assessors and samples, discussed above. However, careful consideration should be given to the design of the experiment, or the evaluation of these effects using analysis of variance may be misleading.

Factorial designs and analysis of variance

Analysis of variance can be used to look at the variation contributed by each of the factors specified in designing the experiment. For example, if different levels of three ingredients have been built into the design, then the effect of these on a particular sensory attribute can be evaluated. Depending on the original factorial design, it is possible to measure the interaction between the ingredients and this effect on a particular sensory attribute.

Reducing the dimensionality of the data and looking at the relationships between samples and attributes

Descriptive data collected on more than two attributes are multivariate by nature and there are statistical methods which can take into account the information provided by all these attributes. The following describes a number of multivariate methods which are commonly used in sensory analysis. Common to all of them is the fact that graphical representation of the data is obtained.

What multivariate methods?

Martens *et al.*, (1983) covers many of the multivariate methods.

Principal component analysis (PCA; Chatfield and Collins, 1980) is a method that derives new independent dimensions (principal components) which are linear combinations of the original attributes. These dimensions are selected to maximize the variation explained, and describe the relationship between samples and attributes in a few underlying sensory dimensions. This method is suitable for conventional profile data.

Generalized Procrustes analysis (GPA; McEwan and Hallett, 1990) has a similar objective to PCA, but takes account of differences in the use of scales and attributes by members of a panel. It is probably the only applicable procedure for free-choice profile data, though it is also worthwhile using GPA for conventional profile data as it allows individual differences between assessors to be evaluated.

Factor analysis (FA; Chatfield and Collins, 1980) has a similar objective to PCA, but is usually based on an underlying statistical model. As such, it is possible to determine the number of significant underlying factors in the data. When applying factor analysis the user should check the assumptions underlying the factor model. Factor analysis is based on the correlation structure between the attributes, and hence factors are formed when high correlations occur with groups of attributes.

Correspondence analysis (CA; Lebart *et al.*, 1984) is a form of PCA which was developed to handle ordinal and frequency-type data. As its name suggests it is ideal for examining directly the association between samples and variables. Since in effect CA performs a PCA on the sample by attribute matrix, and another PCA on the attribute by sample matrix, simultaneous graphical representation of samples and attributes is a direct result of CA.

Discriminant analysis (DA; Chatfield and Collins, 1980) is used to classify samples into groups. It selects the linear combination of attributes which best differentiates between the samples, and as such is useful for evaluating attribute differences between groups of samples. However, the sensory analyst often does not know in advance how the products are going to group, and hence techniques such as PCA are useful prerequisites. DA assumes that the data are multivariate normal, and this assumption should be checked before proceeding.

Canonical variate analysis (CVA; Chatfield and Collins, 1980) derives new independent dimensions in such a way as to describe differences between groups of observations (samples). It does this by maximizing the ratio of between-sample variation to within-sample variation.

Cluster analysis (Chatfield and Collins, 1980) is a method which aims to cluster observations (samples) into different groups. There are many different forms of cluster analysis, and choosing the one to use is not easy. The robustness of selected clusters can be checked using classification techniques (e.g. DA, CVA).

5.2.5 Which methods are appropriate for acceptance tests?

Paired-comparison (preference) test

The analysis is based on the fact that there is a one-in-two chance of choosing either sample by chance. Thus, to say that one sample is preferred, more than half the population must prefer it. Tables, such as those in O'Mahony (1986), can be used to save manual calculation. This is a two-tailed test, as the direction of preference is not known in advance.

Simple visual representation

Graphical methods such as histograms, line graphs and spider diagrams are very useful for examining the shape of the data. For example, histograms may show that the data are skewed, illustrating that the majority of consumers have rated the acceptability of a sample in a similar way. Groupings of consumers on the like and dislike part of a hedonic scale are also apparent as maxima on the histogram.

Exploratory statistics

Medians and the inter-quartile range provide a measure of location and spread of the data. Box-and-whisker diagrams can be used to represent these measures visually (Velleman and Hoaglin, 1981).

Is one sample preferred to the other?

If ratings of acceptability have been collected for two samples, then it is possible to test for differences between the medians of the two samples. If the data for the two samples have been collected from the same consumers, then a paired Wilcoxon signed rank test is used. If different consumers were used to collect the data for the two samples, then a Mann–Whitney U test should be used.

The Wilcoxon test is the nonparametric equivalent of the two sample t-test for related data, while the Mann–Whitney test is the non-parametric equivalent of the two-sample t-test for unrelated data (O'Mahony, 1986).

Are the medians of more than two samples different?

To test if the median acceptability of more than two samples is different, then a Kruskal Wallis test can be used. This is equivalent to a one-way analysis of variance. Using this test, different consumers can be used for each sample (O'Mahony, 1986).

Ranked acceptability data

If the acceptability data have been collected by ranking more than two samples, then a Friedman ranked analysis of variance can be used. This is a two-way analysis of variance which can be used to evaluate differences between samples and consumers (O'Mahony, 1986).

Individual differences in acceptability

Internal preference mapping (MacFie and Thomson, 1988) is used to derive a perceptual map of a number of samples (at least five) based on the acceptability data alone. It also indicates the direction of increasing preference for each individual used in the analysis. This information is often useful for segmentation purposes.

5.2.6 Which methods are appropriate for relating data?

Two dimensional plots are a useful way of examining the shape (nature) of the relationship between two variables.

For example, a plot of preference against storage time may yield a linear relationship suggesting a decline in preference over time. Or a plot of preference against increasing sweetness in a drink may indicate a quadratic relationship (i.e. preference increases with increasing sweetness up to a point, and then starts to decrease).

Correlation coefficients measure the strength of the linear relationship between two variables, and indicate whether this relationship is positive or negative. A positive relationship indicates that one variable is increasing linearly with another variable. A negative relationship indicates that one variable is increasing linearly with a decrease in another variable. Correlation between two variables does not imply cause and effect.

Simple linear regression analysis allows the parameters defining the linear relationship between two variables to be calculated. *Quadratic regression analysis* performs the same job for a quadratic relationship. *Multiple linear regression, principal-component regression* and *partial least-squares regression* are all ways of relating a set of independent variables (e.g. sensory attributes) to one or more response variables (e.g. acceptability measure).

These procedures are particularly useful for relating data sets, such as sensory and chemical data. Care should be exercised with multiple linear regression because of the high correlation which may occur between the independent variables.

External preference mapping refers to a number of statistical models which are used to map acceptability data from consumers on to a profile space of the same samples derived from a multivariate method such as PCA or GPA. There are essentially two types of model: the *vector model* and the *ideal-point model*. The *vector model* represents each consumer as a direction of increasing preference on the profile space (Chapter 10). The *ideal point model* locates the position of each consumer's ideal product on the profile space. In practice, the user of preference mapping has to decide which model is most appropriate for his data (Schiffman *et al.* 1981).

5.2.7 Hypothesis testing

In statistical inference testing a hypothesis is put forward, and the object of the test is to evaluate the chances that two or more products are truly different. In testing whether there is a difference two hypotheses are put forward: the *null hypothesis* (H0) and the *alternative hypothesis* (H1). In a simple example, the null hypothesis states that two products are the same. However, two critical points to note are that two products are never the same and the null hypothesis can never be accepted. The alternative hypothesis states that the two products are different, and if sufficient evidence exists H0 is rejected in favour of H1. Another useful point to note is that statistical significance is, in fact, a statement about the likelihood (or unlikelihood) of the null hypothesis according to the evidence presented by the data.

In statistics there are two types of error associated with hypothesis testing. Type I and Type II. A *Type I error* occurs if the null hypothesis is rejected when it is true, while a *Type II error* occurs if the null hypothesis is accepted when it is false.

Statisticians use the Greek letters α and β to refer to the probabilities of committing these errors.

α = probability of committing Type I error
β = probability of committing Type II error

The power of the test is the ability of the test to reject H0 when it is false, and this is denoted by $(1-\beta)$. Ideally, $(1-\beta)$ should be as near 1 as possible.

Decision	H0 is true	H0 is false
Accept H0	No error $(1-\alpha)$	Type II error (β)
Reject H0	Type I error (α)	No error $(1-\beta)$

The level of α is specified by the person conducting the experiment, and is equivalent to the level of significance. The size of α and β will reflect the seriousness attached to making each type of error. If Type I and Type II errors are equally serious then the values of α and β should be near equal. Obviously the more observations which are collected the more confidence in the results and the greater the chance of keeping β small for a given small α.

5.2.8 Points to consider in choosing a statistical package

Choosing a statistical package is not an easy task as there are so many available, particularly with the increasing use of personal computers (PCs) in industry (see Bibliography).

The first question to be asked is what type of data analysis is planned, and whether this is likely to expand to more complex analysis methods later. User-friendliness is important, particularly for those with limited experience of statistical packages. For example, the non-statistician would find packages such as GENSTAT and GLIM difficult to work with.

The most comprehensive statistical package available for both mainframe computers and PCs is probably SAS, which is suitable for both the experienced and inexperienced statistical user. However, this package is expensive, and one may have to ensure a large number of users to justify the expenditure.

MINITAB may not be as comprehensive as SAS, but nonetheless has significantly expanded its facilities since it was originally introduced. MINITAB Version 7 (1990) provides all the simple exploratory and summary statistics and a comprehensive range of univariate parametric and non-parametric tools, as well as principal-component analysis and discriminant analysis. It is available both for mainframe computers and PCs, is not considered to be expensive and is very user-friendly.

Other packages which are available for the mainframe and PC are SPSS and BMDP. These offer a wider range of multivariate methods than MINITAB, but are more expensive to purchase.

Other packages for the PC include STATGRAPHICS and RS/1, both with similar facilities to MINITAB, and both at a comparable cost. SENSTAT and SENPAK are two PC packages developed and used in the UK which have been designed specifically for sensory analysis. While both these are particularly useful for routine analysis of data, they limit the freedom of the user to explore the data fully.

As a word of warning, a computer's ability to run analyses will depend on the space restraints imposed by the package. However, it is more likely that the storage and data-processing capacity of the PC will be the limiting factor determining the size of data set which can be analysed.

Putting sensory **6** analysis into practice

6.1.1 Are suitable equipment and facilities available?

Before planning a sensory test, ensure that all the necessary equipment is at hand, particularly if preparation is required prior to serving samples. Typically, one would need access to a conventional oven and hobs, microwave oven, refrigerator, freezer and food processor. It is always advisable to ensure that your equipment is standardized or calibrated if at all possible. It is essential to ensure that differences are not introduced in the preparation of the product, which will be wrongly attributed as sample differences in the analysis.

Ideally, the sample-preparation area should be near to the testing area. If it is not, then attention must be given to transporting the samples and maintaining the correct serving temperatures. It is also essential that assessors do not have access to the preparation area, particularly when samples are being prepared or laid out prior to analysis. Assessors will be easily influenced, consciously or subconsciously, by visual clues about the samples.

6.1.2 What are the requirements of the test area?

The requirements for a test area depend upon a number of factors, such as the frequency of testing, the need to 'lay out' large numbers of samples and the requirement to store samples under controlled conditions prior to testing. The allocated area should comfortably accommodate a panel of around 10–12 assessors, plus the panel leader. If larger trials are required, for example with triangular tests or consumer tests, these can often be split into a number of sittings.

It is essential that the room used is suitable for sensory analysis. It should always be available when required, and should be kept free of any strong odours. A conference or meeting room which doubles as a sensory testing room may have the lingering smell of coffee or cigarette smoke which would interfere with the sensory testing. A separate sensory analysis facility has a beneficial effect on panel performance, as permanent improvements can be made to minimize bias. The lighting, for example, can be adjusted to ensure constant light intensities, and fluorescent tubes of the right specification can be installed. In the UK, 'north light' or 'artificial daylight' is recommended as the most appropriate for sensory laboratories where visual observations are required, although the use of special light cabinets is an acceptable alternative.

Coloured lights should be installed to mask colour differences which could introduce visual bias, particularly during difference tests. They are often mounted in booths as light intensities and colours can be more easily adjusted from test to test.

Booths are a useful method of segregating assessors and preventing bias due to group interaction. Companies who carry out routine or regular sensory analysis will benefit from permanent booth installations, particularly if computerized data registration is installed. Otherwise, simple booths can be constructed on a table using wooden dividers. It is usually preferable for analyses to be carried out in booths rather than 'round table'.

Ventilation of the test area is also recommended to maintain constant temperatures and to remove product odours. If positive ventilation is installed, consideration needs to be given to the position of the air intake pipe. This must be positioned so that it will not bring strong odours into the test laboratory from the surrounding area.

6.1.3 What equipment will be needed during sample analysis?

The equipment required will be dictated largely by the form of the samples e.g. glass or cups, plates, bowls, etc. Pottery, glass or disposable utensils can be used depending upon the temperature and nature of the product. Plastic cups or utensils can give off odours and may impart taint to the product under test. Plastic equipment should therefore be avoided if possible. All containers must, however, be identical in any one session. If glass or pottery utensils are used, they should be thoroughly cleaned with a food-grade detergent before use, and kept solely for the purpose of sensory analysis. When coding containers, avoid the use of marker pens which give off strong odours.

6.1.4 Will assessors be available for the test?

Questions related to assessors and assessor availability are covered in detail in Chapter 4.

6.2.1 Product availability and ageing constraints

6.2 Constraints

How much product is available for testing?

Constraints on amount of product may be due to raw material supply and/or processing factors. A restricted amount of sample will affect experimental design; for example, it may require a reduction in replicates (section 5.1.2).

Product shelf-life

This will affect the frequency of tasting in both 'one-off' assessments and storage studies, which in turn affects the organization of panel workloads. Clearly, short shelf-life products are subject to faster deterioration and change than long shelf-life products.

6.2.2 Time constraints

Is there a deadline for completion?

Time constraints will affect the amount of experimentation possible and the detail of the data produced. Always ensure that tests can be comfortably completed within the allowable timescale.

How long will a session take?

This will depend on many variables, including type of test, number of samples, number of replicates, type of product and availability of assessors. Experience will help in judging how long each session will take.

6.2.3 Cost constraints

What level of resource is necessary for the planned testing?

This will depend on the type of testing to be conducted, the frequency of the tests and whether a special panel of assessors is to be recruited. Invariably and unfortunately, sensory analysts often have to select the most appropriate procedures to fit a budget, rather than the other way around. In all cases, a test protocol should never be attempted if it is known that this can only be carried out poorly with the amount of resource available. Always select the simplest test to answer the objective.

What is the cost of setting up the test facilities?

The cost of setting up sensory facilities is usually included in a capital-expansion programme for companies, and it is highly unlikely that the cost will have to be offset against a single project. Establishment costs will obviously vary depending upon the sophistication of the facilities, but adequate facilities with simple booths can usually be provided at modest cost. It is always better to operate well in adequate facilities than poorly in good facilities. Sound and reproducible results will give confidence in the abilities of the sensory panel, and this should eventually lead to investment in facilities to make the operation more efficient. The initial expense of establishing a sensory facility is soon outweighed by the savings made from the information it provides.

In organizing and carrying out a sensory test, the following practical steps are required:

1. From the overall experimental design, draw up a worksheet which contains information on the product, the procedure, date, sample identification/codes, the method of preparation and the order of presentation to individual assessors. The worksheet will be invaluable both in carrying out the test and in writing the final report.
2. Having decided the method of preparation, calculate the amount of time required, allowing plenty of time for preparation prior to the start of the panel session. In most instances (unless the nature of the product demands it), assessors will become impatient if they have to wait more than a few minutes for samples.
3. Calculate the amount of product required and make sure you will have enough to complete the test. Include some extra sample just in case it is necessary.
4. Code the containers to be used by the assessors and lay them out for filling/presentation. Sample codes can be two-, three- or four-digit codes which for most cases can be taken from tables of random numbers, or appropriate letters. In all instances it is important to avoid using codes which imply some pre-defined order or quality. For example, samples coded 1, 2, 3 and 4 would clearly imply a pre-defined order.
5. Code the record sheets to ensure mistakes are not made by the assessors and that order of presentation is maintained. If a computer data-registration system is used, ensure that it is correctly set up for the appropriate trial.
6. Prepare the assessment area for the assessors, providing palate cleansers, cups, pencils, etc. to ensure the test will run smoothly.
7. Prepare the samples and check that the sample requirements in section 3.1.1 are met before calling the assessors to carry out the test. In practice, it is desirable and easier to alert assessors in advance giving them a specific time

for attendance. Advance warning also allows them to fit the test into their own work programme. It is likely that some reminders will need to be given, but it may be easier than trying to recruit a panel while the samples are waiting.

6.4 Assessor briefing and motivation

6.4.1 Do the assessors know what to do?

Instructions should be given or reinforced before testing sessions. Reminders or special instructions should be given immediately before testing.

Background information about the samples may bias assessors' judgements and should not be given until the trial is complete. In all cases, samples must be assessed under code. Assessors should be fully briefed on the test procedure before each testing session, and a common understanding of all relevant descriptors must be established prior to analysis, especially if conventional profiling (QDA) is being conducted.

6.4.2 Do assessors receive feedback on the test results?

Feedback should only be given when a piece of work is complete to prevent the introduction of bias during analyses. Feedback on individual performance is best done cautiously. Positive feedback obviously helps to motivate and boost morale. Negative feedback should be made constructively with, for example, the offer of additional training to ensure that problems are overcome. Helping assessors to improve on their weaknesses requires tactful handling.

Payment or reward may be offered to the assessors as an incentive, but in most companies assessors usually accept the task as 'part of the job'. Special incentives, such as raffles, may be used to encourage regular attendance at panel sessions.

Reporting and **7** recording

A report serves a number of functions. It communicates the results of the exercise to the client, or the manager, and provides a record of the procedure and results. Accurate reporting is essential as it is the basis on which decisions are taken. The intention of this chapter is to suggest a possible report format which will ensure that the important elements of any trial are at least considered in presenting or preparing verbal or written reports. It is understood that all reports need not contain the detail of information suggested, and much will depend upon the circumstances under which the report is given.

Reports can be presented and prepared in a number of ways, but the author should always use the medium most appropriate to the situation. In general, complex data are better represented in graphical form as they are more easily assimilated by the reader, or by the audience if the report is presented verbally. In preparing reports on sensory tests and procedures, the sensory analyst should particularly consider the following points.

Who is the report aimed at?

7.1 Style and content

It is important to define the person, or the department, that will take action as a result of the report, as different reports will be prepared according to use. The way in which the results are communicated will depend upon the ultimate user, and it is likely that several different reports could result from one piece of work. In all cases, the report should be clear and easily understood by the client.

What type of report is required?

Reports should preferably start with a brief but comprehensive summary. The decision must be made as to whether a technical or non-technical report is required, and the degree of expertise of the technical people involved. In most cases, it is unlikely that the client has as much knowledge of sensory analysis as the author, and this will affect the amount of detail required in the report.

Is it necessary to reference any literature?

References which give readers an opportunity to read further into the subject can often be quoted to support statements in the report and can be usefully included where the detail is interesting, but not essential. It is particularly important to reference one's own work, especially if it has some bearing on the results of the research.

If references are quoted in the report then they should be listed as an appendix so that they do not obscure the main purpose of the text. In some reports a bibliography may be required, which differs from a list of references in that it is not confined to publications cited in the text.

7.2 Background and objectives

Why was the work carried out?

The introduction to the report normally includes comments on the circumstances which led up to the work. If so, this should state clearly whether the work was part of an ongoing programme of research or whether it was a repeat of, or similar to, a previous study. The objectives and what the study was intended to answer should be stated clearly, concisely and unequivocally.

What were the constraints?

Any constraints or limitations in the study ought to be mentioned in the introduction as these often have a major influence on the reasons for selecting a particular approach.

7.3 Methods

Which sensory techniques were used?

It is usual to describe the sensory techniques used, adding as much detail as is appropriate and necessary for the reader. The reasons for selecting a particular sensory test in preference to others may be relevant, particularly if its use was a divergence from normal company procedures.

Experimental details

Details of the experimental design may be relevant and, if so, the reasons why this design was chosen should be given. For example, the design may have been selected because of unusual constraints of time and cost. It is important to give details on how many people took part in the experiment, their level of training, and if appropriate how they were selected, how they were obtained, e.g. within or outside company, and any demographic and/or geographic details relevant to the selection of the assessors. Details should be given of the location of tests, whether they were home placement, central location (hall) or laboratory tests. Any specialist facilities used should be mentioned, e.g. tasting booths, lighting conditions, temperature control, air conditioning, or serving utensils, and the report should specify any preparation instructions including recipes, cooking procedures, quantities and holding times, and who prepared the samples.

Details of the instructions given to the assessors, how the samples were identified to the assessors and how many samples they received at one time may also be relevant, as well as the type of mouth cleansers provided, the timing between samples and the temperature (or other factors) of the samples.

Data-collection method

The data-collection method should be specified: for example, face-to-face interviewing, self-completion questionnaire, electronic data collection or tape/video recording. It is often useful to include a copy of the questionnaire in the appendix of the report.

Data format

Data may be used as collected, or modified as necessary to the appropriate format for analysis. Any modification, including grouping of data, should be stated: e.g. category

**7.4
Analysis of data**

to numeric, or normal transformation grouping of non-numeric data, such as open-ended questions. Missing data and any estimations made as a result of this should be stated with reasons.

Statistical methods used

It is often appropriate to refer to the statistical method or methods used, with details appropriate to the reader's needs. It is not usually necessary to give the statistical formulae or the detailed analysis, but if required, these could be put in an appendix.

7.5 Presentation of results

What results should be presented?

Key data must be presented in a suitable form for the reader. Other analyses which have been carried out may be mentioned, but should not be detailed in the body of the report. They may be attached in an appendix if judged appropriate. Original data are not usually presented in the body of a report but are summarized in graphs, diagrams or tables, or described by statistics in the text. There are a number of computer programs designed to produce diagrams, graphs, etc., and these are a good source of the selection available (Bibliography).

Can comments be included/presented?

Comments given in sensory testing can often provide important information. If numbers permit, these statements can be summarized in shortened form, analysed and/or categorized. Any person collating comments should be experienced in this so that the comments are not misinterpreted. If only a small number of comments are given these can be quoted verbatim. Key words appearing in comments sections can be counted to give a rough 'quantitative' measure of the nature of the products.

7.6 Interpreting the data and discussion of results

In interpreting the data and discussing the results, the focus is on what has been established in respect of the original objectives, and should therefore be a consideration of the results leading naturally to the main conclusions. Emphasis should be given to discussions of what has been established and not to a restatement of numerical data. Consideration also should be given to further analyses: whether the data explained the original hypothesis, whether there is a new hypothesis which explains the data better, the degree of confidence in the findings, whether the test/design was effective, whether there were any tendencies which needed highlighting and whether all statistically significant results were likely to be of interest.

What are the key points?

7.7 Conclusions

The conclusions pull together the findings into clear summary statements. They do not rediscuss the findings.

7.8 Recommend- ations

The feasibility of making recommendations will depend largely on the nature of the original briefing. If included, they should state suggested action: they may also indicate any future work needed to fulfil objectives or investigate new areas arising as a result of the work.

Should the data be kept?

7.9 Retaining records

It is advisable to keep the data until the report is approved by the initiator. New questions may arise where data need to be consulted. Before disposing of any data, consult relevant Codes of Practice, e.g. MRS Code of Conduct (1988).

Normal practice is to keep the data in the original format with the appropriate level of security. For convenience, data may also be kept in computerized form, with due regard to appropriate legislation on computer records of data related to individuals (Savage and Edwards, 1984).

Case history: 8
Shelf-life studies

Question: How long can a product be stored before the sensory characteristics change? How do products change with storage?

Background

Since the market introduction of a chocolate-coated filled bar, Future Confectionery Ltd have utilized some new raw ingredients, and their process methods have been adjusted to take advantage of developing process technology. They believe that these changes may have had an advantageous effect on the shelf-life of the product which they wish to confirm in a shelf-life study before authorizing changes to the 'best before' date marking.

Methods and approaches

In order to determine how long the bar can be stored before the sensory characteristics change, it was decided to use a series of triangular tests at periods throughout the shelf-life. To monitor changes in the characteristics of the product over time, conventional profile analysis (QDA) was used, as this provided measurements of the many attributes contributing to the character of the product.

To create a set of samples for the study, sufficient product was taken from one production run, and normal quality assurance tests were performed to ensure that this product was of typical or standard quality. An experimental design had been worked out, taking into account the number of sample dates, the number of assessors, the number of replicates and the need for control samples. From the experimental design, it was possible to calculate the number of samples required to complete the study.

To generate the experimental samples, half of the samples taken from the production run were frozen. Previous work had shown that freezing the product did not affect the sensory quality when thawed, and prevented changes in the sensory quality of the product over time, at least for the period of the study. These samples were subsequently used as control samples.

The remaining samples were stored under ambient conditions and allowed to age for the normal shelf-life duration and beyond. At each designated storage time, a triangular test was performed comparing the ambient stored with the frozen stored sample. Subsets of the samples were taken at periods throughout the ambient storage and placed in the freezer, thereby halting further changes in sensory quality. This procedure was used to build up a range of samples for profile analysis (from the same process conditions and raw material stock) with controlled age increments. In both cases, particular emphasis was given to selecting samples with age characteristics around and beyond the normal shelf-life, as this study was designed to identify whether an extension to the normal shelf-life could be claimed.

Analysis and presentation of results

The analysis of the results of the triangular tests was carried out using the precalculated tables, to determine whether statistically significant differences occurred between test and control samples. The results indicated how long the bar could be stored before changes in the sensory characteristics became statistically significantly different from the control sample.

For the conventional profile analysis, analysis of variance was used to identify attributes exhibiting significant differences within the sample set. The mean intensity values of attributes with significant difference were plotted against age to highlight any trends.

From the results of the profile analysis, it was possible to identify the nature and magnitude of the changes in the sensory characteristics over time, and to make a company decision as whether these changes were acceptable, and whether they represented an extension to normal shelf-life for the product.

Case history: 9
Product matching

Question: Does the sample match the target profile?

Background

Future Biscuits Ltd were moving to a new factory as part of their modernization programme. A new process line had been installed to produce their highly successful malted-milk biscuit, but changes in the processing conditions were inevitable, as much of the existing equipment was either inefficient or obsolete and difficult to replace. With such a strong brand image in a fast-moving market, retaining the sensory characteristics of the biscuits was seen as a primary objective in retaining market share. It was necessary, therefore, to ensure that the new line produced biscuits that had no perceivable sensory differences from the existing production.

Methods and approaches

Company knowledge suggested that the factors most likely to affect sensory characteristics of biscuits were ingredient quality, mixing process and temperature and conditions within the oven.

Ingredient quality, however, was not included in this study as both process lines were supplied from the same stock of raw materials. To cover the ranges of the remaining process factors adequately, samples were produced on the new line to represent three levels of mix and three oven temperatures. Samples of 'standard condition', reflecting process parameters on the old line, were also produced. Samples produced on the old line were used as the target samples.

All samples were evaluated by a trained panel using conventional profile analysis. The data were collected through a computerized data-capture system giving immediate availability for analysis.

Analysis and presentation of results

Analysis of variance of each attribute was carried out, taking account of the process factors, to highlight significant differences and interactions.

'Spider' plots were drawn (Figure 2), and the sensory profiles were compared by overlaying the plots to highlight differences between samples. It was thus possible to identify the process conditions on the new production line which resulted in product that closely matched the standard made on the old production line.

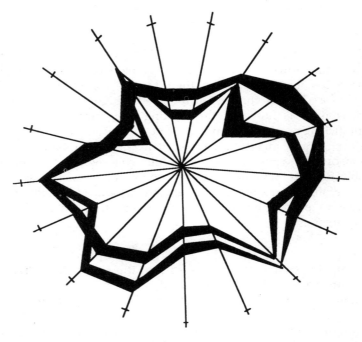

Figure 2 'Spider' plots. Each attribute forms the radius of a circle. The mean and confidence interval of each attribute is plotted for each sample (the thickness of the line (bands) represents the confidence interval either side of the mean). Samples can be compared by overlaying 'spider' plots. If bands overlap there is no significance between the two samples of that attribute. If bands do not overlap, there is a significant difference between the two samples of that attribute.

Case history: **10** Product matching achieved through product mapping

Question: Which combinations of attributes comprise a consumer's ideal product?

Background

Ingredient substitution and flavouring play an important role in formulating cost-effective and acceptable products. This study illustrates that, by considering the relationship between sensory attributes and consumers' liking of samples, Future Drinks Ltd found it possible to manipulate ingredient substitution to maximize product acceptability.

Future Drinks Ltd had observed the consumer trend towards selecting products which were perceived as being more healthy and less fattening. They also saw that the number of intense (non-nutritive) sweeteners available had expanded the potential market for non-sucrose sweetened soft drinks. They realized, however, that in substituting one ingredient for another, particular attention had to be paid to the sensory characteristics of the product. They were particularly worried that the additional sensory attributes associated with intense sweeteners might well be undesirable in some of their products.

In soft-drink manufacture, both single sweeteners and mixtures of sweeteners could be used. Mixtures would normally comprise an intense sweetener and a bulking sweetener (e.g. sucrose) to maintain the mouth-feel characteristics of the drink. Future Drinks Ltd were particularly interested in investigating a new intense sweetener which was reputed to have a 'clean' sweetness and which did not leave the bitter after-taste associated with other intense sweeteners. One of their objectives, therefore, was to determine the combination of sucrose and sweetener most acceptable to the consumer. They chose to work initially on carbonated cola, as this was their major line both as a standard and low calorie product.

Method and approaches

Nine samples of cola drink were formulated and manufactured in the pilot plant. Colas sweetened with the sweetener, sweetener–sucrose mix and sucrose, were formulated with three strengths of cola flavouring to complete a factorial design.

Sensory analysis was seen as the most important element in this product-optimization programme. The nine samples of cola were described by a panel of ten trained sensory assessors, using the technique of free-choice profiling. Hedonic ratings on the same nine samples were also collected from 112 consumers, selected from Future Drinks Ltd's Household Consumer Panel, according to their age, social class and usual cola consumption, the object being to collect data from a representative cross-section of the consuming population.

Analysis and presentation of results

The company sensory analyst was asked to make a presentation on the findings of this study so that a suitable strategy for the future could be developed.

In the free-choice profiling, assessors used between 9 and 14 attributes to describe the nine samples of cola. The data were submitted to generalized Procrustes analysis (GPA) to derive a perceptual representation of the samples. A two-dimensional sample configuration was derived from the GPA (Figure 3), and this explained 70% of the total variation in the data. Correlations between the principal axes and each of the original attributes were calculated and this showed the first dimension separating the colas according to strength of flavour. The second dimension separated the samples according to sweetening type. The hedonic data were analysed to determine if there were any overall differences in acceptability between the samples. Three samples were significantly more liked than the other six samples.

To relate the data from the sensory and acceptability

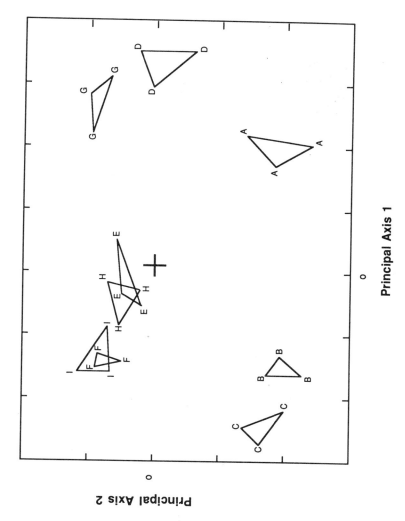

Figure 3 Two-dimensional consensus space of the nine cola samples. Replicate positions are indicated by the formation of a triangle.

trials, external multi-dimensional preference mapping was used to map individual's hedonic data on to the sample space derived from generalized Procrustes analysis using the vector model (Schiffman *et al.*, 1981). In this particular experiment, the vector model (Figure 4), was fitted by 71 consumers. Many of the preference vectors were in the direction of the four samples in the top-left quadrant of the plot.

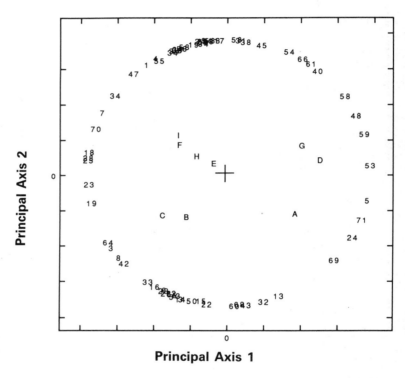

Figure 4 Vector-preference mapping model for 71 consumers. Lines drawn from the origin represent the direction of increasing preference for each numbered consumer.

It was clear to Future Drinks Ltd that the majority of consumers preferred samples with characteristics associated with the top left-hand quadrant, and that future product positioning should be directed to this aim. The analyses also confirmed that the sensory attributes associated with the second dimension had the most influence on cola acceptability and that subsequent product alterations which changed these attributes would have a greater influence on acceptability than those characterizing the first sensory dimension.

Case history: **11**
Taint investigation

The sensory analyst at Future Confectionery Ltd was asked to determine the answers to the following questions, about suspected taint in new confectionery lines of boxed chocolates.

- *Is there a detectable difference in odour/flavour from the standard?*
- *How is the odour/flavour described and how strong is it?*
- *In addition, information was needed on the source of the taint.*

Future Confectionery Ltd had built up a stock of the new **Background** boxed confectionery item and stored it before launch in a store controlled by another company. On launch, complaints were received of an unpleasant off-flavour in some of the chocolates in the box.

The sensory analyst investigating the problem asked questions of the relevant departments and established the following background information:

- Freshly manufactured product was untainted.
- Stored samples were tainted.
- Not all the items in a box were tainted.
- Tainted items were not found in all boxes.
- Stored pallets had been dismantled so location of boxes/ tainted items were not known.
- All product had been removed from store, and only one store had been used.

- Although the store was not controlled by Future Confectionary Ltd, it had been checked before use.
- Earlier controlled storage trials had not indicated any problems.

Methods The sensory analysis department was located at a central facility and samples of freshly manufactured product were despatched for analysis. Examples of tainted product were sent in a separate parcel to avoid the possibility of cross-tainting.

No reports of any ill-effects of tasting the tainted product had been received, and it was agreed that it would be safe to taste small quantities using a panel of expert assessors. These assessors had wide experience in taint analysis and the ability to give good written descriptions of flavour characteristics. Ensuring that the control and test samples were well separated at all times, products were analysed and a full set of descriptors of the taint odour and flavour obtained.

Interpretation of written comments both by the sensory analyst and an analytical chemist indicated the classes of chemical compounds which might be implicated in the taint problem, and samples were submitted for confirmatory chemical analysis. Against a very complex background, certain esters were identified as possible sources of taint, but conclusive proof that they were the cause of the taint could not be established.

Simultaneously, the sensory analyst had taken steps to try to determine the source of the taint, but checks on all steps in the manufacturing operation including any solvents used on or near the line were inconclusive. Odour tests on the packaging material were clear, and no taint was detected in product stored with packaging material in glass containers at elevated temperatures for one week.

Checks were also made on visiting the store, and an extremely faint estery aroma was detected briefly on entry. Investigation of the activities of other businesses around the store, especially in the direction of the prevailing wind, gave no clues as to the possible source of the taint.

However, in view of the odour clue in the store, the sensory analyst set up a trial to expose slices of mild butter in the store on glass plates for 72 hours. The butter for the test was sliced in a clean environment in the Sensory Analysis Department, and both exposed and unexposed butter were subjected to the same travel and temperature.

Assessing both control and exposed butter using the expert panel gave sensory descriptors of taint to the exposed sample which were very similar to the descriptors used to describe the taint in the original tainted product, and the sensory findings were supported by further chemical analysis. Having established the probable source of the taint, further chemical tests (drawing in-store air over adsorbent material and later desorbing it) were set up which again confirmed the sensory findings.

Results

Discussions with the store manager and examination of the store records helped to identify the likely original source of taint and the chemical tests further confirmed this. As a result revised procedures were issued by Future Confectionery Ltd to cover use of stores which were not under their direct control. In this instance sensory analysis had:

- confirmed the presence of the taint;
- indicated the likely classes of chemical compounds;
- eliminated from the search some sources of taint;
- pinpointed the source of taint.

Case history: **12**
Taint prevention

Future Confectionery Ltd want to paint a production bay with a low odour paint. The sensory analyst was asked the following questions:

- *Will the paint cause taint in sweets manufactured in the production area?*
- *Is it necessary to stop production for painting, and if so, for how long?*

The conditions of use were established as follows: **Background**

- Two walls 8 m high totalling 30 m long were to be painted; the volume of the bay was 1600 m³.
- Ventilation was low, as there is a need to keep high humidity and temperature in the bay.
- Only one product was at risk. The time from raw materials emerging from the process vessel to leaving in packed boxes was 50 min.

A specific test was designed in which the sweets were **Methods** exposed in small scale conditions approximating to the in-use situation.

A container of known volume was selected, into which about 20 sweets were placed. A sheet of foil, painted with the low-odour paint, was laid in the container. The area of foil was such that the area:volume ratio approximated to in-use conditions. The foil was left in the container for 75 min, which equated to the normal exposure time with a safety factor included. The container position and lid position were chosen to simulate the ventilation conditions in the bay.

At the same time, a control was set up in which the full set of test conditions were repeated without the paint on the foil, great care being taken to ensure there was no cross contamination of the samples. When the exposure time was over, both exposed and control samples were collected and stored in glass jars.

A panel of trained assessors was used to rate both samples for taint intensity on a 100 mm line scale, with the scale from no taint to strong taint. Samples were coded, and a specified and balanced taste order was used. Both odour and flavour taints were rated by the panel.

A panel of 8–12 assessors was used and the differences between ratings for control and test were computed and subjected to a t-test where the null hypothesis stated that the mean difference rating was zero and the alternative hypothesis stated that the mean difference was greater than or less than zero. In the first instance non-rejection of the null hypothesis was required, but individual responses were noted. If an individual detected a taint, then those assessors were asked to repeat the test after an interval. If that individual was consistent in determining a taint, then the paint was rejected, or stringent conditions for its use were documented.

This procedure tested the effect of painting during production. The second, alternative painting regime was to paint the bay during the weekend, when all raw material and product had been cleared from the site. If this was done, production would need to restart approximately 38 hours later.

A second test was set up in which the painted foil was not put into the test container until the paint on the foil had been cured for 38 hours.

Results   In this case the null hypothesis was rejected on the test of fresh paint, but not rejected on the test of paint after 38 hours curing when no assessor detected a taint. It was therefore recommended that the bay should be painted during the weekend, and production not restarted until 38 hours had elapsed after completing the work.

Whilst many approximations were made in the procedure many potential problems had been avoided. Doubtless using this procedure several satisfactory products may have been rejected, but Future Confectionery Ltd were satisfied, as no taint problems had been reported using products which had passed the test.

Case history: 13
Specification and
quality control

Question: What is the target specification and how can it be defined?

Future Drinks Ltd were receiving a high level of consumer complaints about their new range of flavoured milk drinks relating to the sensory qualities of appearance and flavour.

A study of the methods being used to monitor and control the quality highlighted a lack of coordination, consistency and standardization in the methods used. Principally, there was no clear quality specification or coordinated methodology document available for operators to refer to and operators were, therefore, making their own judgements on product quality. As a consequence, their results were not consistently recorded or fed back into the system for use in improving control of the quality in any way.

The first task was to create a quality specification which included a clear and precise methodology, covering microbiological, physical and sensory aspects of the product.

Future Drinks Ltd had always adhered to the statutory health and safety regulations with regard to the process and handling of their products and were confident that they were producing a safe product. The relevant acceptable ranges of each aspect measured were written into the main body of the specification and the designated methods and practices into the 'methods to be used' section. Clearly, however, the company had failed to make a product which satisfied the consumer.

Previous market research had identified the attributes and levels important to the consumer and it was from this that the product had been formulated and produced. Similar sets of samples were therefore evaluated by the trained panel to produce a list of representative terms which characterized the product. Using these terms a sensory specification was written with accept/reject ranges for each attribute.

Programme introduction   To ensure effective monitoring of production quality, all operators were screened for their sensory abilities, and the critical operators trained to identify the acceptable range of normal production variation. With regular monitoring of assessors, and strict on-line quality control checks with feedback into the system, Future Drinks Ltd soon saw a dramatic reduction in their consumer complaint rate.

Appendix:
Some useful tables
for sensory tests

The following tables were derived using the MINITAB statistical package.

Table A1. The number of assessors in a paired comparison or duo-trio test required to give correct judgements, at three different significance levels (one-tailed test) Note: not valid for preference

Number of assessors	Significance level		
	5%	*1%*	*0.1%*
5	5	–	–
6	6	–	–
7	7	7	–
8	7	8	–
9	8	9	–
10	9	10	10
11	9	10	11
12	10	11	12
13	10	12	13
14	11	12	13
15	12	13	14
16	12	14	15
17	13	14	16
18	13	15	16
19	14	15	17
20	15	16	18
21	15	17	18
22	16	17	19

Table A1.   *continued*

Number of assessors	Significance level 5%	1%	0.1%
23	16	18	20
24	17	19	20
25	18	19	21
26	18	20	22
27	19	20	22
28	19	21	23
29	20	22	24
30	20	22	24
31	21	23	25
32	22	24	26
33	22	24	26
34	23	25	27
35	23	25	27
36	24	26	28
37	24	26	29
38	25	27	29
39	26	28	30
40	26	28	30
41	27	29	31
42	27	29	32
43	28	30	32
44	28	31	33
45	29	31	34
46	30	32	34
47	30	32	35
48	31	33	36
49	31	34	36
50	32	34	37

Table A2 The number of assessors in a triangular test required to give correct judgements, at three different significance levels.

Number of assessors	Significance level 5%	1%	0.1%
5	4	5	
6	5	6	–
7	5	6	7
8	6	7	8
9	6	7	8
10	7	8	9
11	7	8	10
12	8	9	10
13	8	9	11
14	9	10	11
15	9	10	12
16	9	11	12
17	10	11	13
18	10	12	13
19	11	12	14
20	11	13	14
21	12	13	15
22	12	14	15
23	12	14	16
24	13	15	16
25	13	15	17
26	14	15	17
27	14	16	18
28	15	16	18
29	15	17	19
30	15	17	19
31	16	18	20
32	16	18	20
33	17	18	21
34	17	19	21
35	17	19	22
36	18	20	22
37	18	20	22
38	19	21	23
39	19	21	23
40	19	21	24
41	20	22	24
42	20	22	25

Table A2.   *continued*

Number of assessors	Significance level 5%	1%	0.1%
43	20	23	25
44	21	23	26
45	21	24	26
46	22	24	27
47	22	24	27
48	22	25	27
49	23	25	28
50	23	26	28

Glossary of terms used in sensory analysis

In most cases, contributors to these *Guidelines* have used nomenclature as defined in the International Standard *Sensory analysis – Vocabulary* (ISO, 1990). Extracts from International Standards are reproduced with permission. Complete copies can be obtained through national standards bodies and readers should refer to these documents for definition of terms not covered in this summary.

Acid (taste): Describes the primary taste produced by dilute aqueous solutions of most acid substances (e.g. citric acid and tartaric acid).

After-taste: Olfactory and/or gustatory sensation which occurs after the elimination of the product, and which differs from the sensations perceived whilst the product was in the mouth.

Appearance: All the visible attributes of the food.

Assessor: Person taking part in a sensory test.

Attribute: Perceptible characteristic.

Bias: Systematic errors which may be positive or negative.

Bitter (taste): Describes the primary taste produced by dilute aqueous solutions of various substances such as quinine and caffeine.

Comparative assessment: Comparison of stimuli presented at the same time.

Confidence (statistical): The limits within which the true value of a population parameter is stated to lie with a specified probability, e.g. 95% confidence.

Consumer: Person who uses a product.

Contrast effect: Increase in response to differences between two simultaneous or consecutive stimuli.

Control: Sample of the material under test chosen as a reference point against which all other samples are compared.

Convergence effect: Decrease in response to differences between two simultaneous or consecutive stimuli.

Detection threshold: Minimum value of a sensory stimulus needed to give rise to a sensation. The sensation need not be identified.

Difference test: Any method of test involving comparison between samples.

Difference threshold: Value of the smallest perceptible difference in the physical intensity of a stimulus.

Discrimina-tion: Act of qualitative and/or quantitative differentiation between two or more stimuli.

Duo-trio test: Method of difference testing in which the control is presented first, followed by two samples, one of which is the same as the control sample. The assessor is asked to identify the sample which is the same as the control.

Error (of assessment): The difference between the observed value (or assessment) and the true value.

Factorial design: An experimental design where all the factors included are measured.

Hedonic: Relating to like or dislike.

Independent assessment: Evaluation of one or more stimuli without direct comparison.

Magnitude estimation: Process of assigning values to the intensities of an attribute in such a way that the ratio of the value assigned and the assessor's perception are the same.

Objective method: Any method in which the effects of personal opinions are minimized.

Off-flavour: Atypical flavour often associated with deterioration or transformation of the product.

Off-odour: Atypical odour often associated with deterioration or transformation of the product.

Paired comparison test: Method in which stimuli are presented in pairs for comparison on the basis of some defined attributes.

Panel: Group of assessors chosen to participate in a sensory test.

Perception: Awareness of the effects of single or multiple sensory stimuli.

Preference test: Test to assess preference between two or several samples.

Profile: The use of descriptive terms in evaluating the sensory attribute of a sample and the intensity of each attribute.

Quality: Collection of features and characteristics of a product or service that confer its ability to satisfy stated or implied needs.

Qualitative analysis: Describing the nature of the product.

Quantitative analysis: Measurement of perceived amount of each attribute in the product.

Question-naire: A form having a set of questions designed to obtain information.

Ranking: Method of classification in which a series of samples is placed in order of intensity or degree of some specified attribute. This process is ordinal with no attempt made to assess the magnitude of the differences.

Rating: Method of classification according to categories, each of which is placed on an ordinal scale.

Recognition threshold: Minimum value of a sensory stimulus permitting identification of the sensation perceived.

Respondent: Person taking part in a consumer test.

Reference: Substance, different from the material under test, used to define an attribute or a specified level of a given attribute.

Replicate: To evaluate a sample more than once.

Salty (taste):   Describes the primary taste produced by aqueous solutions of various substances such as sodium chloride.

Sample: (i) A product type.
                      (ii) One piece for evaluation.

Scale:

Continuum, divided into successive values, which may be graphical, descriptive or numerical, used in reporting the level of a characteristic.

Scale (hedonic):

Scale expressing degrees of like or dislike.

Scale (interval):

Scale where numbers are chosen in such a way that equal numerical intervals are assumed to correspond to equal differences in sensory perception.

Scale (ordinal):

Scale where points are arranged according to a pre-established or continuous progression.

Scale (ratio):

Scale where numbers are chosen in such a way that equal numerical ratios are assumed to correspond to equal sensory perception ratios.

Scoring:

Method of evaluation of a product or of the attributes of a product by means of scores (having a mathematical significance).

Screening:

Preliminary selection procedure.

Sensory:

Relating to the use of the sense organs.

Sensory analysis:

Examination of the sensory attributes of a product perceptible by the sense organs.

Sensory fatigue:

Form of sensory adaptation in which a decrease in sensitivity occurs. Sensory adaptation is a temporary modification of the sensitivity of a sense organ due to continued and/or repeated stimulation.

Subjective method:

Any method in which the personal opinions are taken in consideration.

Sweet (taste):   Describes the primary taste produced by aqueous solutions of various substances such as sucrose.

Taint: Taste or odour foreign to the product.

Triangular test: Method of difference testing involving the simultaneous presentation of three coded samples, two of which are identical. The assessor is asked to select the sample perceived as different.

Variables: Factors which are changed under experimental control.

Source: ISO 5492–1: 1977, ISO 5492–2: 1978, ISO 5492–3: 1979, ISO 5492–4: 1981, ISO 5492–5: 1983 and ISO 5492–6: 1985.

Bibliography

Amerine, M.A., Pangborn, R.M. and Roessler, E.B. (1965) *Principles of Sensory Evaluation*, Academic Press, New York.

ASTM (1968a) *Basic Principles of Sensory Evaluation*. Special Technical Publication No. 433, American Society for Testing and Materials, Philadelphia.

ASTM (1968b) *Manual on Sensory Testing Methods*. Special Technical Publication No. 434, American Society for Testing and Materials, Philadelphia.

ASTM (1968c) *Correlation of Subjective–Objective Methods in the Study of Odors and Tastes*. Special Technical Publication No. 440, American Society for Testing and Materials, Philadelphia.

ASTM (1973) *Compilation of Odor and Taste Threshold Values Data*. DS No. 48, American Society for Testing and Materials, Philadelphia.

ASTM (1976) *Correlating Sensory Objective Measurements*. Special Technical Publication No. 594, American Society for Testing and Materials, Philadelphia.

ASTM (1979) *Manual on Consumer Sensory Evaluation*. Special Technical Publication No. 682, American Society for Testing and Materials, Philadelphia.

ASTM (1981) *Guidelines for the Selection and Training of Sensory Panel Members*. Special Technical Publication No.

758, American Society for Testing and Materials, Philadelphia.

Ball, A.D. and Buckwell, G.D. (1986) *Work Out Statistics: 'A' Level*. MacMillan, London.

BSI (1975) *BS 5098: Glossary of Terms Relating to Sensory Analysis of Foods*. British Standards Institution, London.

BSI (1982) *BS 5929: Methods for Sensory Analysis of Foods. Part 2: Paired Comparison Test*. British Standards Institution, London.

BSI (1984) *BS 5929: Methods for Sensory Analysis of Foods. Part 3: Triangular Test*. British Standards Institution, London.

BSI (1986a) *BS 5929 Methods for Sensory Analysis of Foods. Part 1: General Guide to Methodology*. British Standards Institution, London.

BSI (1986b) *BS 5929 Methods for Sensory Analysis of Foods. Part 4: Flavour Profile Methods*. British Standards Institution, London.

BSI (1989) *BS 5929 Methods for Sensory Analysis of Foods. Part 6: Ranking*. British Standards Institution, London.

Cairncross, E.E. and Sjostrom, L.B. (1950) Flavor profiles: A new approach to flavor problems. *Food Technology*, **4** (8), 308–11.

Chatfield, C. (1983) *Statistics for Technology*. Chapman and Hall, London.

Chatfield, C. and Collins, A.J. (1980) *Introduction to Multivariate Analysis*. Chapman and Hall, London.

Cochran, W.G. and Cox, G.M. (1957) *Experimental Designs*. John Wiley, New York.

Danzart, M. (1986) Univariate procedures, In: *Statistical procedures in Food Research*, ed. J.R. Piggott. Elsevier Applied Science, London, pp 19–59.

EOQC (1976) *Glossary of Terms Used in Quality Control*, European Organisation for Quality Control.

Fransella, F. and Bannister, D. (1977) *A Manual for Repertory Grid Technique*, Academic Press, London.

Gacula, M.C. and Singh., J. (1984) *Statistical Methods in Food and Consumer Research*, Academic Press, London.

Gower, J.C. (1975) Generalized Procrustes analysis. *Psychometrika*, **40** (1), 33–51.

Greenbaum, T.L. (1988) *The Practical Handbook and Guide to Focus Group Research.*, Lexington Books, Toronto.

Harper, R. (1972) *Human Senses in Action*, Churchill Livingstone, Edinburgh.

HMSO (1984) *Food Labelling Regulations*. Statutory Instrument No. 1305. Her Majesty's Stationery Office, London.

HMSO (1988) *Health and Safety: Control of Substances Hazardous to Health Regulations*. Statutory Instrument No. 1657, Her Majesty's Stationery Office, London.

HMSO (1989) *Food Labelling (Amendment) Regulations*. Statutory Instrument No. 786, Her Majesty's Stationery Office, London.

HMSO (1990) *Food Labelling (Amendment) Regulations*. Statutory Instrument No. 2488, Her Majesty's Stationery Office, London

Ishihara, S. (1967) *Tests for Colour-Blindness*, Kanehara Shuppan Co. Ltd, Tokyo.

ISO (1979) *Sensory Analysis – Determination of Sensitivity of Taste.*, ISO 3972.

ISO (1990) *Sensory Analysis – Vocabulary*. ISO/DIS 5492/ DAM (Draft)

Jellinek, G. (1985) *Sensory Evaluation of Food: Theory and Practice*, Ellis Horwood, Chichester.

Jowitt, R.J., (1974) The terminology of food texture. *Texture Studies* **5**, 351–58

Kapsalis, J.G. (1987) *Objective Methods in Food Quality Assessment*, CRC Press, Florida.

Kramer, A. and Twigg, B.A. (1970) *Quality Control for the Food Industry*, AVI Publishing Company, Connecticut.

Land, D.G. and Shepherd, D. (1988) Scaling and ranking

methods, in: *Sensory Analysis of Foods*, 2nd edn, (ed. J.R. Piggott), Elsevier Applied Science, London, pp 115–85.

Langron, S.P. (1984) *The Statistical Treatment of Sensory Analysis Data*. PhD Thesis, University of Bath.

Lebart, L., Mirineau, A. and Warwick, K.M. (1984) *Multivariate Descriptive Analysis: Correspondence Analysis and Related Techniques for Large Matrices*, Wiley, New York.

Lyon, D.H., McEwan, J.A., Taylor, J.M. and Reynolds, M.A. (1988) Sensory quality of frozen Brussels sprouts in a time–temperature tolerance study. *Food Quality and Preference* **1** (1), 37–41.

MacFie, H.J.H. and Thomson, D.M.H. (1988) Preference Mapping and Multidimensional Scaling. In: *Sensory Analysis of Foods*, 2nd edn, (ed. J.R. Piggott) Elsevier Applied Science, London pp. 381–409.

Malik, H.J. and Mullin, K. (1973) *A First Course in Probability and Statistics*, Addison-Wesley, London.

Market Research Society (1988) *Code of Conduct*

Martens, H., Wold, S. and Martens, M. (1983) A layman's guide to multivariate data analysis. In: *Food Research and Data Analysis*. (ed. H. Martens and H. Russwurm, Jr.). Applied Science Publishers, London.

McEwan, J.A. (1989) *Statistical Methodology for the Analysis and Interpretation of Sensory Profile and Consumer Acceptability Data*. Technical Memorandum No 536, CFDRA, Chipping Campden.

McEwan, J.A. and Hallett, E.M. (1990) *A Guide to the Use and Interpretation of Generalized Procrustes Analysis*, Statistical Manual No. 1. CFDRA, Chipping Campden.

McEwan, J.A., Colwill, J.S. and Thomson, D.M.H. (1989) The application of two free-choice profile methods to investigate the sensory characteristics of chocolate. *Journal of Sensory Studies*, **3** (4), 271–86.

Meilgaard, M., Civille, G.V. and Carr, B.T. (1987) *Sensory Evaluation Techniques*. Vols I and II, CRC Press, Florida.

MINITAB (1990) *Minitab Reference Manual – Release 7*, Minitab Inc., Pennsylvania, USA

Moskowitz, H.R. (1977) Magnitude estimation: notes on what, when and why to use it. *Journal of Food Quality*, **3**, 195–228.

Moskowitz, H.R. (1983) *Product Testing and Sensory Evaluation of Foods: Marketing and R & D Approaches*. Food and Nutrition Press, Connecticut.

Moskowitz, H.R. (1985) *New Directions for Product Testing and Sensory Analysis of Foods*, Food and Nutrition Press, Connecticut.

Neave, H.R. (1989) *Statistics Tables*, Unwin Hyman, London.

O'Mahony, M. (1986) *Sensory Evaluation of Food: Statistical Methods and Procedures*, New York: Marcel Dekker, Inc., New York

Oppenheim, A.N. (1966) *Questionnaire Design and Attitude Measurement*, Gower, Aldershot.

Passmore, R. and Eastwood, M.A. (1986) *Human Nutrition and Dietetics*, Churchill Livingstone, London.

Peryam, D.R. and Pilgrim, F.J. (1957) Hedonic scale method for measuring food preferences, *Food Technology*, **11** (9), 9–14.

Piggott, J.R. (1986) *Statistical Procedures in Food Research*, Elsevier Applied Science, London.

Piggott, J.R. (1988) *Sensory Analysis of Foods*, Elsevier Applied Science Publishers, London.

Poulton, E.C. (1989) *Bias In Quantifying Judgements*, Lawrence Erlbaum Associates, London.

Savage, N. and Edwards, C. (1984) *A Guide to the Data Protection Act*, Financial Training Publications, London.

Schiffman, S.S., Reynolds, M.L. and Young, F.W. (1981) *Introduction to Multidimensional Scaling: Theory, Methods and Applications*, Academic Press, New York.

Spiegel, M.R. (1972) *Theory and Problems of Statistics*. Schaum's Outline Series, McGraw-Hill, New York.

Stone, H. and Sidel, J.L. (1985) *Sensory Evaluation Practices*, Academic Press, London.

Stone, H., Sidel, J., Oliver, S., Woolsey, A. and Singleton, R.C. (1974) Sensory evaluation by qualitative descriptive analysis. *Food Technology*, **28** (11), 24–32.

Thomson, D.M.H. (1988) *Food Acceptability*, Elsevier Applied Science, London.

Velleman, P.F. and Hoaglin, D.C. (1981) *The Applications, Basics and Computing of of Exploratory Data Analysis*, Duxbury Press, Boston.

Williams, A.A. and Atkin, B.A. (1983) *Sensory Quality in Foods and Beverages – Definition, Measurement and Control*, Ellis Horwood, Chichester.

Williams, A.A. and Langron, S.P. (1984) The use of free-choice profiling for the evaluation of commercial ports. *Journal of the Science of Food and Agriculture*, **35**, 558–68.

Williams, A.A. and Arnold, G.M. (1985) A comparison of six coffees characterized by conventional profiling, free-choice profiling, and similarity methods. *Journal of the Science of Food and Agriculture*, **36**, 204–14.

Wolfe, A.R. (ed.) (1984), *Standardised Questions: A Review for Market Research Executives*. Market Research Society.

Statistical Packages

BMDP	BMDP Statistical Software, Cork Technology Farm, Model Farm Road, Cork, Ireland. BMDP Statistical Software Inc., 1440 Sepulveda Blvd, Los Angeles, CA 90025, USA.
GENSTAT	NAG Ltd, Wilkinson House, Jordon Hill Road, Oxford OX2 8DR, Great Britain.
GLIM	NAG Ltd, Wilkinson House, Jordon Hill Road, Oxford OX2 8DR, Great Britain.
MINITAB	CLECOM Ltd, The Research Park, Vincent Drive, Edgbaston, Birmingham, B15 2SQ. Minitab Inc., 3081 Enterprise Drive, State College, PA 16801, USA.

RS/1	BBN UK Ltd, Software Products Division, One Heathrow Boulevard, 286 Bath Road, West Drayton, Middlesex UB7 0DQ, Great Britain. BBN Software Products, Marketing Communications, 10 Fawcett Street, Cambridge, MA 02138, USA.
SAS	SAS Software Ltd, Wittington House, Henley Road, Medmenham, Marlow, Bucks SL7 2EB, Great Britain. SAS Institute Inc., Box 8000, SAS Circle, Cary, NC 27511–8000, USA.
SENPAK	Reading Scientific Services Ltd, Lord Zuckerman Research Centre, Whiteknights, PO Box 234, Reading RG6 2LA, Great Britain.
SENSTAT	Sensory Research Laboratories Ltd, 4 High Street, Nailsea, Bristol, BS19 1BW, Great Britain.
STATGRAPHICS	Statistical Graphics Corporation, 5 Independence Way, Princeton Corp. Ctr, Princeton, NJ 08540, USA. Cocking and Drury Ltd, 180 Tottenham Court Road, London W1P 9LE, Great Britain.
SPSS	SPSS UK Ltd, 9–11 Queens Road, Walton-on-Thames, Surrey KT12 5LU, Great Britain. SPSS Inc., 444 North Michigan Avenue, Chicago, IL 60611, USA.

Index

Page numbers in *italic* represent figures, numbers in **bold** represent tables.